ABOUT THE EDITORS

JESSICA VINCENT is a multi-award-winning travel journalist whose work has appeared in *National Geographic Traveller*, *BBC Travel*, *Condé Nast Traveller* and many more. Jessica is the Global Travel Media Alliance Global Travel Writer of the Year and the Travel Media Awards Young Writer of the Year. She writes about disappearing traditions, culinary cultures and adventures with social impact. Find her on Instagram @nomada.travel.

LEVISON WOOD is a British explorer, writer and photographer who has produced several critically acclaimed documentaries and published nine bestselling travel books, including *Walking the Nile*, *Walking the Himalayas* and *Walking the Americas*. He is a Fellow of the Royal Geographical Society and the Explorers Club.

MONISHA RAJESH is a British travel writer and journalist. She is the author of *Around India in 80 Trains*, *Around the World in 80 Trains* (winner of the National Geographic Traveller Book of the Year in 2020 and Shortlisted for the Stanford Dolman Award), and *Epic Train Journeys*.

SIMON WILLMORE (twitter.com/SiWillmore) is a travel journalist and the youngest-ever Chairperson of the British Guild of Travel Writers. He has written for magazines such as *Wanderlust*, contributed to books for Rough Guides and Frommer's, and is the Digital Manager of Bradt Guides.

THE BEST BRITISH TRAVEL WRITING OF THE 21ST CENTURY

This paperback edition published in 2023
First published in hardback in 2022

An Hachette UK Company
www.hachette.co.uk

Summersdale Publishers Ltd
Part of Octopus Publishing Group Limited
Carmelite House
50 Victoria Embankment
LONDON
EC4Y 0DZ
UK

www.summersdale.com

Printed and bound by CPI Group (UK) Ltd, Croydon, CR0 4YY

ISBN: 978-1-80007-996-0

Substantial discounts on bulk quantities of Summersdale books are available to corporations, professional associations and other organisations. For details contact general enquiries: telephone: +44 (0) 1243 771107 or email: enquiries@summersdale.com.

Every effort has been made to trace copyright holders and to obtain their permission for the use of copyrighted material. The publisher apologises for any errors or omissions and would be grateful if notified of any corrections that should be incorporated in future reprints or editions of this book.

EDITED BY

JESSICA   LEVISON   MONISHA   SIMON
VINCENT   WOOD   RAJESH   WILLMORE

THE BEST BRITISH TRAVEL WRITING

OF THE 21ST CENTURY

A CELEBRATION OF OUTSTANDING TRAVEL
STORYTELLING FROM AROUND THE WORLD

BGTW
BRITISH GUILD of
TRAVEL WRITERS

battle**face**®

CONTENTS

FOREWORD

BY JESSICA VINCENT

I was in Bulgaria when everything changed. The air smelled of pinewood and charred meat; my hands were burning with cold. It was March 2020 and I was spending the month writing, skiing and eating paprika-spiced *bobchorba* in Bansko, a wood-and-sheepskin village at the edge of the Pirin Mountains. On that perfect bluebird morning I'd planned to ski Todorka Peak and eat garlic bread straight from a clay oven, but I knew something was wrong before I reached the front of the gondola queue.

"Not today," a stern-faced woman said with a wave of her candy-pink acrylic nails. "Mountain closed."

It was, of course, inevitable. The coronavirus had reached Europe, and non-Bulgarian nationals were to leave immediately. With no home of my own in the country I belonged to, I would spend the next three months – the longest I'd spent anywhere in the last four years – living at my in-laws' in the tiny East Anglian village of Boxted.

Rural Essex felt worlds away from my life on the road. I went from trekking through jungles in Mexico and ice climbing in Peru to doing downward dogs and baking cakes on repeat within the same four whitewashed walls. The full-time traveller in me felt trapped. The writer in me, unable to see past the fog of familiarity and routine, was void of ideas to pitch to editors. I didn't have it bad compared to many, but I did fear for my job – because what is a travel writer who can't travel?

I couldn't travel, but I *could* read. As infection numbers rose, I'd lose myself in the words, and worlds, of others. I'd smell the cigarette smoke of Tibet's Qinghai railway with Monisha Rajesh; I'd walk the scorched fields of southern Spain with Laurie Lee; I'd listen to the note of a broken piano in the Siberian tundra with Sophy Roberts. The adventure didn't stop there: magazines like *National Geographic Traveller* and *Sidetracked* took me on food trails through Hanoi and rock-climbing expeditions in China.

The more I read about travel from a locked-down world, the more I realised that I'd got it all wrong. There was a time when I thought of travel as going to faraway places and seeing as much as possible, as if tallying up hundreds of countries and monuments would somehow make me a wiser, worthier traveller. But the more I read, the clearer it became: the essence of travel isn't to move – it's to *feel*.

With that, I hung up my baking tray and went in search of wonder close to home: I foraged my local woods for nettles and wild garlic; I paddled the length of the River Stour in a blow-up kayak; I walked sections of the longest coastal path in the world, taking time to smell the grass and taste the salt of the North Sea. For the first time in my life, I looked at my home as I would any other country: with curiosity and a sense of adventure. I hadn't left home, but I was finally travelling again.

It was out of this strange, but enlightening, time that *The Best British Travel Writing of the 21st Century* was born. Amid a climate of closed borders and fear for the outside world, I wanted to compile a book that celebrates the stories and writers that for the past two decades have made us *feel* something for the unknown and, in the process, brought us closer to it. As I hope this anthology shows, the best travel writing won't just make you want to go somewhere, it'll make you want to *know* it.

To ensure as many people as possible were given the chance to be part of this book, I asked writers from around the world to submit up to three of their favourite travel stories published in UK magazines, newspapers or online journals between 2000 and 2021. My co-editors – three hugely respected writers in the travel-writing space – and I chose the final collection based on the quality of the writing, originality and their ability to inspire and educate readers.

We were particularly mindful of diversity, too: you'll notice that the collection includes a range of voices, writing styles and destinations. The result is a book where stories on racism, religion and identity are heard side by side, and where countries like Italy and Britain rub shoulders with Iraq and Pakistan. This is a book that celebrates the beautifully crafted and thoughtfully researched travel narratives of the last 20 years, but it also looks to the future – to a brighter, more inclusive era of travel writing.

Choosing "the best" of anything, especially something as subjective as travel writing, comes with its own challenges – some might even say it's futile. But to celebrate no one out of fear of choosing inadequately seems equally pointless, and perhaps even a little cowardly. These stories were chosen not just because they inspire wanderlust, but because they confront important, and sometimes uncomfortable, issues like climate change and the exploitative nature of travel. I ask you to approach this anthology as you would any other travel narrative: with an open mind and a willingness to fall in love with the world, and the people in it, all over again.

Wherever you are and whatever travel means to you, I hope this book inspires you to get out into the world. Whether you're backpacking Southeast Asia or camping in your local woods, I hope you'll go in search of wonder not to tick off sights or to take a photo for social media, but to listen, to learn and, most importantly, to *feel*.

INTRODUCTION

BY LEVISON WOOD

Travelling – it leaves you speechless, then turns you into a storyteller.
Ibn Battuta

I've always felt a strong connection to these famous words by Ibn Battuta. In the 14th century, the Moroccan adventurer travelled for thirty years all around the known world, venturing further than any other explorer in pre-modern history.

I studied his journeys while I was at university and was compelled by this notion. I could think of nothing better than having the ability to share big ideas – to travel and to tell stories. And so I have – I've been lucky enough to visit over 100 countries and make a career out of spending a life on the road.

This inherent connection between travel and storytelling is written into our DNA. Storytelling has been at the heart of human communication long before even languages developed. Cave drawings dating back 30,000 years, found in Lascaux in France, show artistic representations of animals and people in motion. Two thousand years ago, the ancient Greek geographer Pausanias wrote one of the very first discovered travel guides, focusing not on the practicalities of the journey like where to stay or what to eat, but on the identity and history of Greece, and the landscapes, local myths and artworks that he saw.

To me, Ibn Battuta's words represent the immense power of travel to open ones eyes to the important stories of the day;

to help you connect with people that you otherwise might not come across. It gives you new perspectives and the ability to continue to learn about the world. Travel changes who you are, and in my opinion, it makes you a more understanding and compassionate person.

This notion is something that has become part of my essence – the opportunity that travel affords you to grow, learn and evolve. Yet, in the wake of the coronavirus outbreak, the ability to jump on a plane at the drop of a hat suddenly disappeared. Without that exhilarating feeling that I got from travelling far and wide, and all the lessons that I thought I could only learn from exploring, I felt a gaping hole – a troubling loss. It seemed that the world spun a curveball and we all forgot to duck.

It was a whole new world to navigate, and even home felt strangely foreign with new rules and restrictions. We began to speak a new language: of working from home, lockdowns and quarantines. I felt claustrophobic.

But then I stopped. I thought. I tried to approach this new existence in a way that I would a new journey. What can we learn from this experience? What lessons can we take with us when the world opens up again? I started to think about storytelling and what inspired me to travel in the first place.

And so, I delved back into my bookshelf and re-read the diaries of Captain James Cook. I pored over Wilfred Thesiger's exploits in the deserts of Arabia and laughed at the feigned amateurishness of Eric Newby and Hugh Carless as they bumbled over the Hindu Kush. I turned to travel magazines and newspapers for inspiration. Stories, some of which are included in this book, took me far and wide, learning lessons that I would never get from my own travels; lessons I could only gain from these writers' unique experiences, perspectives and from that moment in time. From Ash Bhardwaj's journey to India to take his dad's ashes to the holy Ganges River, I learned about the power of travel to connect you with your heritage. Lilly and Andrew Ryzebol took me to the dark otherworldly depths of Lake Huron's Georgian Bay to learn how facing a lifelong fear and pushing your limits can bring purpose and meaning to life.

All of a sudden, I had that feeling again. That buzz. This was it – the very reason *why* I started to travel in the first place. To learn and to look in wonder at the magic of the world.

Now that I can travel again, I've realised that this reflection on *why* I travel has given me a new appreciation and understanding of it. Sometimes you don't realise how important something is to you until you lose it. In our busy lives, it's easy to get caught up in the moment and forget the very reason for doing something we love. Writing is inherently about reflection. When Jess approached me and asked me to edit this book, it felt like the stars had aligned. She too had taken comfort in the arms of great travel storytelling at a time when actual travel was out of reach.

As I'm sure you will agree, travel writing is a genre of huge importance. Yet it has changed dramatically since the tales of ancient explorers. It is no longer about documenting unchartered territories or mapping newly discovered lands. Now that people have been almost everywhere, it might seem that travel writers have lost their purpose.

But when you consider the wide-ranging subject matter contained in this anthology, it becomes apparent that travel writing has evolved into a crucial way of engaging with your place in the world in a particular moment. It's about understanding your experience. Travel writing is slow. It disregards the fast news cycle and takes a step back to observe. It is much more about getting to know a destination, its people, and where you sit among them. It has become a personal response to a place. And in my opinion, this makes it more valuable than ever before.

Now, as the world opens again, remember that being an armchair explorer has the power to make you appreciate your own adventures all the more. I hope that when reading this book, you will see it for what it is: a celebration of genre that can transport you to far-off destinations, one that champions storytelling but is also anchored by reality – the recipe for inspiration. I hope you come away wanting to travel. But I also hope you come away wanting to read more about travel.

To write is to understand, no matter who reads it. Whether you document your journeys in a diary or in a best-seller, the objective is to develop your ideas and thoughts. In the excellent writing in this book, I feel that I am going through experiences with the writers and taking away the lessons that they learned.

Before lockdown, I had only ever thought of Ibn Battuta's quote in its current order. Now I understand a new meaning. Above all, lockdown made me remember that behind every great adventure there are stories that inspired it. So, think of it as more like an incredible, interconnected circle:

*"Reading great travel storytelling – it leaves you
speechless, then turns you into an explorer."*

THE
NIGHT
TRAIN

—

Leon McCarron

For *Suitcase* magazine
October 2020

"I have two families," says Haider Naeem, driver of the night train to Basra. "One is at home in Baghdad. The other is here with me, travelling between these cities."

Standing around him are three companions from the driving crew nodding happily in agreement. One tends to a boiling kettle that rests uneasily beside a cockpit of dials and another heaps pyramids of sugar into squat paper cups. Tinny Bluetooth speakers play slow, mournful songs by Iraqi crooners from the 1970s. Ahead, a narrow ribbon of track, illuminated by the convergence of two brilliant roof-mounted beams, clacks and clicks as it is swallowed beneath us. Beyond is only darkness. Haider's gaze jumps between his smartphone playlist, the control panel and, of course, the view. I am handed a cup of sugar disguised as tea and encouraged to feel at home. "Take a seat," says Haider. "One of the most exciting parts is coming up. This is where the water buffalo like to cross the track."

The passenger train from Baghdad to Basra is all that remains of a one-time rich heritage of rail travel in Iraq. A tram system was replaced in 1914 by an Ottoman track running north from Baghdad, and eight years later the invading British constructed a narrow-gauge line to connect the southern port city of Basra. The year 1940 saw the first-ever continuous journey from Istanbul to Baghdad. The trip took just three days, but it marked the culmination of 30 years of imperial attempts to connect Europe to Iraq via the Turkish capital.

Today, after decades of conflict, occupation and sanctions, most of the railways in the country lie abandoned and skeletal, buried under sand, mud or water. A century has passed since that inaugural journey to Basra by the time I arrive in Baghdad to begin my own. Baghdad Central Station is now the grand starting point for travellers; a vast colonial building that opened in 1953 as the masterwork of British architect J. M. Wilson. "It's like a piece of England in Iraq," a station manager tells me, as I look around. "But with special features for us." An ornate chandelier hangs low from a domed roof in the columned central chamber, and recesses house dilapidated booths that once sold tickets to Turkey and Syria. In a place designed for crowds, empty space has now become the most noticeable feature of all.

The operational trains themselves are a fleet of Chinese models, bought in 2014 by the Iraqi government. Alongside them on the platforms are husks of previous incarnations, including Saddam Hussein's personal carriage – now looted and stripped bare – and another that carried the King. Night travel is the only option these days, in part because the tracks are unprotected and darkness means less chance of people, cars and animals getting in the way.

———————

At 6.15 p.m., when the last light of a winter sky has just faded into the warm glow of Baghdad, we are called to the sleeper train with around 150 other passengers. There are families pulling along suitcases and carrying complications of plastic bags, and soldiers with rucksacks casually flung across their shoulders. No mercy is shown in the rush to board first.

We are three, two foreigners and an Iraqi, and within moments of being installed in our compartment – four beds, a small table and a series of light switches that do nothing to affect the dazzling cabin bulbs – we are visited by Abbas Tamimi who works as a security guard for the train. "If anything goes wrong, I'll jump down and protect the train," he tells me with a wide grin. I ask if that is likely to happen. "No, because the Chinese trains never break down!" comes the response. He brings me along the carriage to meet his sister Hana. They have the same smile. "The train is much safer than the roads," she says. "That's mostly the reason why I take it. Also, I get a cheap ticket because of my brother." They both giggle.

I am visited by two more curious neighbours and, afterwards, I do the same to the others in our carriage. This theme of safety quickly becomes apparent. "The highway is a death trap," says one man, an officer in the Iraqi army. Another says he hears about crashes almost every night. Abbas points out the obvious. "Some people would be worried about security in southern Iraq, but that's not the issue at all. It's bad drivers."

There is a small, sparse dining car, but no one seems to be buying the food. Mostly it functions as the buffer between cabins and seats. Some passengers play backgammon across headrests while others lean in to listen or be heard. The rest lounge, dozing in awkward positions. There is a familiar cadence, I think, to long-distance rail travel, no matter where in the world the train and traveller. This is almost certainly part of the appeal; strangers thrust together in a confined space with shared destinations and limited distractions. Conversations take on the rhythm of the journey, and there are no awkward silences – the cacophony of moving carriages sees to that.

Many on board are young men going back to work after time off in Baghdad. Some are travelling to do paperwork. An elderly woman, Zeinab, takes the train every two weeks to visit her sister. Mohamed is going to pick up a new SUV from the port. Four teenagers somehow snuck on without a ticket. Outside, the city slips away. We move behind gardens and past open windows and it feels a touch voyeuristic, like we're seeing a view of the city that we shouldn't. A girl brushes her teeth and a man smokes on his balcony. A young couple sit on their rooftop beside a palm tree wrapped in fairy lights. Highways come to a halt as we pass and then we are out, beyond the Tigris and into the black. I had hoped to see more of Iraq on the journey, but instead I must be content to be spirited through at night. Somewhere out there are palm groves, the Euphrates, marshlands, but everyone assures me it's better this way; faster, simpler.

"Iraq is complicated," says an engineer called Ali. He has broad shoulders and a weathered face and implores me: "You must understand. It's been broken up into these different parts, but we should all be the same. Travelling in darkness makes it feel like there are fewer problems." Others echo this symbolism of the train as a means of connection. "I hope they rebuild the track to Mosul soon," says a teacher, Fatima. "I think the train should take people to all parts of Iraq, to both Sunni and Shia areas, without checkpoints."

Although the temptation is to look at what's been lost, perhaps it is more productive to focus on what's still there. A soldier, on his way back from a deployment in Anbar, says that everything that remains in Iraq has been hard-won against adversaries hell-bent on destruction. That the train line still connects Baghdad to the south is a success; more victories will follow.

It is later on when we are invited to meet the drivers. As we watch for the buffalo – "look for the glint of their eyes" – Haider says that his job is a service. "I love it because I'm helping. We take everyone. Poor people, rich people, anyone." For a brief time, he says, they are in charge of transporting passengers safely and making it the best experience possible. "Iraqis are friendly," he continues. "The train is one way of bringing us all together, even just for a short time." With that he cuts the lights, then flashes them back on and sounds the horn. "No buffalo tonight," he concludes. "But soon we have another exciting section where there are no barriers on the crossing roads. Would you like to stay?"

AFTER THE FLOOD

—

Oliver Smith

For *Lonely Planet* magazine
October 2016

After 150 days on the water, Noah, his family and all the animals heard a loud CRUNCH as the ark hit dry land. They had arrived on a little island – which, as the waters receded, turned out not to be an island at all, but the tip of an immense mountain. The mountain was called Ararat, and it towered high over a rocky landscape. After some months the world was dry again, and Noah's family and animals descended (many seizing the opportunity to trot off to warmer and/or more exotic parts of the world). But legend tells that Noah's great-grandson, Hayk, stayed put in this stony land, and founded Armenia. It would become the first Christian nation on earth.

After 4,500 years, the biblical deluge has turned to a light drizzle as my plane lands in Yerevan, the Armenian capital, but the importance of Ararat has not been forgotten. At the border control, a guard pauses from playing solitaire on his phone to ink my passport with an Ararat-shaped stamp. Travelling into Yerevan among Soviet-era tower blocks, the taxi passes the stadium of FC Ararat (the Man United of Armenia), and the Ararat Cognac factory. Among the wide boulevards of the city centre are the Ararat Restaurant and the Ararat Hotel – where, according to Tripadvisor, some rooms smell of cigarettes (possibly Ararat-brand cigarettes). In the cafes around the Opera House you can use Ararat-adorned banknotes from the ATM outside AraratBank to buy Ararat Beer and Ararat Wine, excessive consumption of which may mean you're admitted to Ararat Medical Centre. And close by is the clock tower of Government House, which bears the national crest: Ararat etched in stone.

A range of modest-sized peaks surrounds Yerevan, and on cloudy days you might spend some hours working out which one is Ararat. But this is a mistake: seeing the real mountain entails tilting your head a little higher and squinting at the sky until a patch of brilliant whiteness appears – not clouds, but a glimpse of an immense snow-capped summit, wildly out of proportion to everything else in view. On days when it is visible, Ararat is hypnotic in its vastness: taller than any peak in the Alps and most other things this side of the Himalayas.

Ararat stalks visitors to Yerevan: lingering among the laundry lines, playing peek-a-boo behind shopping malls. For millions of Armenians, it is the first thing they see when they open their curtains in the morning, and the last before they go to bed. It is a key to understanding this ancient country.

———————

From Yerevan, I head eastward beneath the lower slopes of Ararat and up into a wind-scoured plateau. The road winds among craggy escarpments and extinct volcanoes. On one mountain pass stands a fourteenth-century caravanserai where merchants would have rested on journeys between Samarkand and Istanbul. Military towers from Soviet Times – windows smashed and satellite dishes broken – still rise like lighthouses over meadows of swaying grass.

Though an independent country since 1991, Armenia has always been a frontier territory: a small nation squished between the superpowers of Persia, Russia and Turkey. Armenia stands on the boundary of Christian and Muslim worlds, the border of the former USSR and the West, and the junction of three tectonic plates too.

Nothing has stood firm through seismic tremors and tides of invaders like the monasteries of the Armenian Apostolic Church – counting among the most ancient Christian structures on earth.

"Armenians build beautiful churches because we are beautiful people," insists Father Sahak Martirosyan. He is the priest of one of the most exquisite monasteries, Noravank, set in a canyon an hour's drive from Yerevan. "Our architects used stones as their words: they were expressing their innermost feelings with their designs."

Father Sahak shows me round the monastery, peeking into churches blackened by years of burning incense, where vines reach through the windows. Pulling back the sleeve of his robe, he taps at his iPhone to show me his pictures of Noravank through the seasons: winter days of deep snowfall when no visitors came; summer evenings walking the forests nearby. He comes to a picture of Ararat taken from a viewpoint not far away, the mountain rising above a bank of cloud, giving the impression it had detached itself from earth and were hovering weightless in the sky.

"Ararat is the symbol of Armenia," says Father Sahak. "It means rebirth, for this is where mankind took its first steps on earth after the flood." I ask him if he believes the Ark is still hidden on Ararat, but he smiles and does not answer.

In its mother cathedral at Echmiadzin, the Armenian Apostolic Church keeps what is said to be a fragment of Noah's Ark, found on the mountain by a fourth-century saint, propped on a Plexiglas stand next to a claimed piece of the True Cross. Countless others have set out for the mountain looking for the Ark without success: maverick priests, NASA astronauts, TV crews. Most recently came the case of Donald MacKenzie, a part-time builder from the Outer Hebrides obsessed with finding the Ark. Telling no one where he was going, he climbed Ararat carrying little more than a tent, a Bible and a small telescope. Donald disappeared, last seen in September 2010 high on the mountain, straying from the main path soon before a storm blew in.

Father Sahak studies the picture of Ararat until the screen dims, and he pockets his phone with a melancholy sigh. It is a sound you hear in Armenia whenever the name of Ararat is spoken. Sometimes the sigh takes the form of a faintly audible tut. Sometimes it is a long, sorrowful gust of breath.

It is the sigh that tells you the symbol of Armenia is not in Armenia at all. It is a few miles over a closed border, in Turkey.

The closest most Armenians come to Ararat is Khor Virap: another monastery, set among the watchtowers marking the Armenian-Turkish border. It stands on a rocky bluff from which you can hear the call to prayer drifting across no man's land when the wind blows east.

Scored into the coarse volcanic rock of the monastery are the names of countless pilgrims who have visited here – including some carved by weak hands precisely one century ago. These particular pilgrims were also refugees, escaping from what many believe was the first genocide of the twentieth century. Historians estimate that up to 1.2 million Armenians were killed by Ottoman armies during the turmoil of the First World War. Millennia-old Armenian communities in the lands west of Ararat – in present-day Turkey – were wiped out by death marches, mass burnings and by forcibly capsizing boats out at sea. When plotting the extermination of ethnic Poles, Hitler was reputed to have said, "Who speaks today of the annihilation of the Armenians?"

The question of the genocide is part of everyday Armenian life, mostly because it is still unresolved. The Ottoman Empire's successor state, Turkey, refuses to apologise for the killings, saying that the deaths were a result of war and not systematic ethnic cleansing. It is for this reason that Turkey and Armenia remain hostile neighbours, and that the border remains closed. It is also for this reason that thousands of pilgrims come to Khor Virap every year to peer over the impassable frontier as if it were a coastal cliff – and to look up the mountain, which is a symbol of everything that has been lost.

There is no coastline in Armenia, nor is there easy access to the sea: as well as a closed border with Turkey to the west, the boundary with neighbouring Azerbaijan is also shut following a war in the 1990s. It means that almost 90 per cent of its land frontiers are blocked: despite being a landlocked country, some say Armenia is as isolated as a Pacific island.

The place locals head for when any claustrophobia sets in is Lake Sevan, known to some as the "Armenian Ocean" – one of the highest freshwater lakes in the world. Seen on a clear day, it is a picture of serenity: snowy ranges mirrored in the still waters of the lake, their crisp reflections sliced in two by little fishing boats out on their morning rounds. Along the shore are resorts from Soviet times, when comrades from Estonia or Siberia came on holiday here. They swam out from pebbly beaches and composed poems to the motherland, watching cloud formations blow over from the Caspian Sea.

And, in a meadow beside the northern shore, is the strangest sight in all Armenia: a mighty seagoing boat, timbers weathered and bruised by Atlantic waves. Look closer, and you might spot its owner: a man with a silver-grey beard and steely-blue eyes, who built this boat himself with no experience, and who keeps it in a field of cows, 300 miles from the nearest sea. But this isn't a sign of an impending deluge. It is one of the great triumphs of twenty-first-century Armenia.

"Like me, Noah was an amateur boatbuilder," says Captain Karen Balayan, sitting in the galley of his ship. "But Noah's boat was a box designed only to float: mine was built to go somewhere!"

An electrical engineer who built model yachts as a youngster, Captain Karen is the president of the AYAS Nautical Research Club: a group of friends who, in 1985, resolved to build a full-sized medieval sailing ship from scratch. The boat was to be called *Cilicia* and would follow a fourteenth-century Armenian design, from a time when Armenians had their own Mediterranean coastline. Karen studied documents in the British Library, soon finding himself bribing foresters with vodka to get the right kind of timbers. He and his crew slept aboard the half-built boat during the collapse of the Soviet Union (to make sure no one chopped it up for firewood), and in 2002 launched her on water for the first time at Lake Sevan.

"It is rather strange being the captain of a seagoing ship in a landlocked country," says Karen. "Perhaps the sea has stayed in my genetics since the days when Armenians were seafarers. Building the boat and taking it onto the ocean was my dream. If you follow your path without deviating, you will achieve your dreams."

Sailing on Lake Sevan was a warm-up act for a far greater odyssey. Standing in the galley, Karen retraces his 2004 route on a faded map torn from an Austrian Airlines in-flight magazine. It started with *Cilicia* being wheeled over the mountains to Georgia's Black Sea coast (to the confusion of traffic police). There followed two years of adventures with a crew of a dozen. They sailed among cargo ships in the Bosphorus and gondolas in the Venetian lagoon, under the battlements of Malta and beneath the Rock of Gibraltar, steering among the dolphin pods of Biscay and beneath the raised arms of Tower Bridge. Finally, they returned from the Baltic to the Black Sea by Russian rivers and canals, becoming the first ever vessel to circumnavigate Europe — all in a medieval boat registered in a landlocked nation. Karen climbs up on deck to show me the oak rudders — snapped in two during one stormy night on the Black Sea, meaning the crew had to steer using saucepans and buckets to stop their ship capsizing.

"We were frightened. After a point instinct takes over, the fear disappears and all you feel is the will to stay alive, to sail on."

This Armenian impulse to travel is nothing new. Armenians have settled in distant corners of the world in a way only comparable with Jews. There is a local joke that Armenians have most likely settled on undiscovered planets. It was an Armenian photographer in London who took the defiant image of Churchill that appears on the new £5 note; an Armenian architect in Istanbul who designed the dome on the Aya Sofya that represents the vault of heaven itself. And it's also true the most googled person in the world is an American woman of Armenian descent: Kim Kardashian. In diaspora communities around the world — California to Calcutta, Buenos Aires to Beirut — Armenian families hang pictures of Ararat on their walls, to remind them of a homeland they might never have visited.

Karen shows me his favourite place on the boat: the captain's perch beside the stern. From here, the cows are hidden beneath the gunwales of the *Cilicia*, and Lake Sevan seems to rise straight from the prow. The distant leagues of the lake vanish into the morning mist, and for the briefest moment there is a sense that Karen might be afloat on endless waters, sailing high above the earth on the boat that he built.

It is only a very brief moment, for it is soon time to go back below deck. It has started to rain again.

ROYAL ENCOUNTER

Solange Hando

For *Real Travel*
February 2009

Kira, pins, belt: it was all there, beautifully laid out on the bed, but how do you put on a Bhutanese dress? Perhaps the hotel staff could help?

"Sorry, madam, there are no ladies on duty at this time."

So I ended up with two men in my room, struggling with metres of fabric, red and gold, folding this way, that way, under the arm, over the arm to no avail. "I can't be late for a coronation," I pleaded, so the youngest ran out into the street to find a woman who knew what to do. Minutes later, I made an almost royal appearance at the top of the stairs.

Like every Bhutanese at home or abroad, I had waited a year and eleven months for this happy occasion, ever since the Fourth King stepped down in favour of his son. But in this small Himalayan kingdom, court astrologers had deemed the coming year inauspicious and the country patiently held its breath in anticipation. When would it be after that? Spring, summer? The date was finally announced, 6 November, and every flight was booked within hours.

After a week of cloud and mist, we woke to clear blue skies and mountains glowing in the rising sun. This was a good sign. A gentle breeze ruffled the willows down by the river and myriad flags fluttered in brilliant colours. Draped in smiling posters of the King, Thimphu, the usually sleepy capital, was all set to celebrate. There were food stalls along the streets, coronation badges and stickers and lots of flags for you to wave, while in the post office, for a limited period, you could buy the first-ever personalised stamps, just pop inside, smile for the camera and there's your face on the stamp. Imagine the surprise when your postcards get home…

A NEW DRAGON KING

In the massive Tashichho *dzong* up valley, the monks had been up long before dawn, offering incense and prayers while three precious Buddhist images were unfurled from the eaves. Fresh pine needles were laid on the ground, rice patterns adorned the red carpet and the first dignitaries filed through the gate, followed by members of the royal family, greeting each other with hugs and kisses, and the President of India, a close ally and only head of state to be invited, minimising costs at the King's request.

We watched in wonder as the glittering Grand Procession graciously escorted His Majesty into the *dzong*. There were musicians on the rooftops, dancers in the courtyard and gifts of silk sashes and ceremonial wine, before the party retired to the private Chamber of the Golden Throne. There, at the most auspicious time of 8.31 a.m., the Fourth King crowned his son, Jigme Khesar Namgyel Wangchuck, in the presence of Je Khenpo, the chief abbot. No sparkling diamonds, only a traditional silk crown embroidered with tantric skulls and a blue raven's head, representing the protective deity, Mahakala. The Fifth Dragon King was blessed with empowering and auspicious offerings, including curd, incense, yellow mustard and a right-whorled conch shell.

Meanwhile, the public was gathering in the nearby Ceremonial Ground, eager to greet this bright new king, the world's youngest reigning monarch, who promised to serve rather than rule. He had already toured the country in its most remote corners but still they came, from every direction, yak herders who had walked for days, old folk carried on horseback, nuns who drew lots for a place on an open truck, so many the new Tendrey Thang could not hold them all. The King decided to extend the celebrations by a day so no one would go home disappointed.

The afternoon was a memorable event, 20,000 people, said the papers, dressed in their finest clothes, *kiras* for the ladies, *ghos* for the men, woven in intricate patterns, brocade, silk, vivid sashes and belts, silver brooches, sometimes a chunky necklace of turquoise and coral handed down through generations. They had dreamed of this day for a long time and planned to look their best. Now all waited for their turn as His Majesty relentlessly worked his way through the crowds, humbly bent in half, blessing children, hugging babies, offering a kind word or a joke, receiving armfuls of *khadars* – auspicious white scarves – and handing everyone a commemorative coin. No rush, no fear, only mutual trust and respect. Draped in red and gold, with traditional boots, sleek black hair and a dazzling smile, the newly crowned king won every heart around.

That night, I dreamed of barefoot dancers and swirling colours, cymbals, drums, bugles and horns and two days of glorious entertainment yet to come. Now that the King had looked into my eyes and said "Thank you for coming", I wanted to see it all.

CELEBRATIONS

I am not too fond of military shows but the morning parade was short and delightful, toylike soldiers marching to perfection and silver bands in knee-length robes and embroidered boots, my favourites raising alternate shoulders in tune with the music like puppets on a string. The King addressed the nation, pledging to "protect his people like a parent, care for them like a brother and serve them like a son", then balloons rose above the stadium, orange, yellow, blue, white, like so many stars floating to eternity.

The little girl next to me shaded her eyes with her flag and beamed with delight.

"Now it's time for *Thri-buel*," said my guide Rinzin, "presents from the people." So here they came, two horses, two yaks, two white sheep, two elephants and a calf, five bales of textiles, nine bags of cereals, three stashes of coins and more. All would be returned to their owners, with a royal blessing, but no one would forget the elephants who had never been seen in Thimphu and raised their trunk to greet the Fifth Druk Gyalpo, the Dragon King.

The Bhutanese love to dance and the coronation was no exception. Schoolchildren had been rehearsing for months to entertain King and Country and showcase the culture of this small but diverse kingdom. In bright simple attire, they took it in turn to celebrate the Beauty of the Land, Gross National Happiness, Peace, Long Life and 100 years of monarchy. There were sacred dances too, Guru Rinpoche and his eight manifestations under a golden umbrella, the Drametsi Drums, the Black Hats ensuring good karma, but most of all, we enjoyed the herders' dance when men dressed up as yaks pounced around the grounds. Now and then, I must admit, the hypnotic rhythm saw me twirling around, as discreetly as I could, in my little corner of the stadium.

The King watched it all, leaving the Royal Pavilion from time to time to greet the VIPs in their ornate tents and people in the sunny stands. Family members followed suite, "*Chu chu*, sit down," they'd say as we stood to show respect and when I raised my camera in front of the royal cousins, they beckoned with a smile, inviting me to pose with them and their lady-in-waiting. That's definitely an auspicious picture, I'll keep it on my desk to make sure I return.

FUN AND GAMES

When it came to the games, I was strictly an onlooker. Where else but in Bhutan would you have a pillow fight to celebrate a coronation? They came in two by two, grown-up men hoisted onto a metal frame, hitting each other with a pillow sack, one blue, one red, until the loser fell in a tub of water below. The King was so amused he strode across the ground for a closer look, laughing at every mighty splash and joining the audience in applause. There were martial arts displays and a hugely popular strong man competition which involved lifting boulders, tyres and logs and racing to the finish with a weight of 250 kilos. On the sidelines, Rinzin was having his own mini-contest, being picked up like a feather, right off the ground, by his friend Sonam. He still looked handsome though, sporting designer sunglasses given by Bruce Parry when he escorted him for BBC *Tribes*. I was in good company.

Meanwhile the archery was in full swing. This is Bhutan's national sport, practised by every man in the land, from toddlers with homemade bamboo bows to world-class champions with state-of-the-art equipment. All was done according to tradition, initial prayers and offerings, victory dance and women in colourful *kiras* lining up at the side, singing to encourage their team or jeering to deter opponents. The royal princes took part, and the King himself who aimed, shot, hopped on one foot and waved his bow like everyone else. Only the first notes of Tashi Lebey, the Farewell Dance, brought the game to an end as the whole stadium came down on the pitch, swaying and shuffling in ever growing circles to wish everyone *"Tashi delek"*, long life and good luck. I caught my last glimpse of His Majesty as he danced in the middle of it all, "strikingly handsome", as said his Prime Minister, and truly the "People's King".

INDIAN PILGRIMAGE: WINDSOR TO THE GANGES

Ash Bhardwaj

For *The Telegraph*
April 2013

I'm trying to concentrate on the gravity of the moment and accurately repeat the Sanskrit words of the priest, but it's hard to ignore so overwhelming a setting.

I'm in Haridwar, north India, sitting on a small square of marble that projects into the rushing River Ganges. Thousands of Indians excitedly splash in the river to cleanse sins, acquire merit and have fun; loudspeakers blare a curious mixture of recorded prayers and security warnings; the smell of incense, spices and hot human flesh fills my nostrils, while the sunlight has the diffuse, liquid richness that I have only ever seen in the subcontinent.

The touch of my sister's hand pulls me back to the present. I turn to look at her, tears streaming down her cheeks, and together we pour our father's ashes into the churning waters, completing a journey that began six years and 6,000 miles away.

Just after I finished university, my father died. On the day of the cremation, my eldest uncle sat me down at my home in Windsor and told me that it was my responsibility to take Dad's ashes to India and perform a ritual known as *Tharpan* – immersing the ashes in the Ganges, under the guidance of a Hindu priest, or *pandit*. According to Hindu belief, the Ganges bridges the mortal and spiritual realms; releasing Dad's ashes there would enable his soul to travel to the afterlife and be reborn.

The idea of taking part in such an important ritual in India was intimidating: I had grown up in Windsor, went to the local comprehensive school and was never taught Hindi or Punjabi by my father. When we were children, our English mother regularly took us to visit our Indian family, but I had been baffled by proceedings at festivals and events. I always felt like a clumsy outsider.

I had, however, long been fascinated by stories of pilgrimage, those great odysseys in which the voyager reaches a destination and undergoes a revelation. In Hindi this is known as a *yatra* and, with my duty in mind, I set out to create my own. It took me six years, from the age of 22 when dad died, to learn enough about my Indian heritage to feel ready to set out on the journey. There was also a second element to this ritual – as a rite of passage, it would mark my transition from boy to man in the eyes of my Indian relatives, and I wanted to make sure I felt ready for it.

Dad had left India in 1962 and set up home in Windsor, where he met and married my English mother. He and I had a difficult relationship, but we'd talked about visiting India together to see the land of his childhood. Before setting off on my *yatra*, I visited the Hindu temple in Southall, where a guardian explained that my father's spirit was still with me, waiting to be released; on the journey, I would have to speak to my father as if he were alive. I came to think that we would be visiting India together after all.

So on a bright spring day, I headed north to the Manchester crematorium where my father's ashes waited. I was nervous, but also felt a sense of enlightened determination – I had a task to do, a mission to accomplish and I felt ready at last. The procrastination, planning and research were over and I was on my way to mystic India.

Arriving in Delhi today, with its gleaming new airport terminal, is a far more pleasant experience than ten years ago, when a fence was the airport's only facility. We stayed at the ITC Maurya, where the butler, Ashok, was enthralled with my story and proceeded to share his extensive knowledge of the saints of India.

"Saint Bhardwaj, from whom you are descended, was a master of the military arts and one of the Seven Great *Rishis* [sages]," he enthused. "Bhardwaj eventually ascended to Heaven and became a star in the constellation that you call the Plough. His descendants became powerful priests and rishis in their own right, as well as great horse-lords and masters of war." It's astonishing to think that millions of Indians invoke my surname each time they point out dots of light in the night sky.

The next morning we set off early along Delhi's newly built motorways, bullock carts and bicycles among the trucks and shiny Land Cruisers. The cityscape faded away to the flat, hazy plains of north India, and before long we were in green-and-beige countryside. A nervous excitement grew in me as we approached Haridwar, like the kind I used to feel before a game of rugby at school.

Arriving at Haridwar – passing stalls piled high with flowers, powdered dye and other offerings to the gods – I immediately felt that I was in a place unlike anywhere in Europe, for the city exists solely for the conduct of religious ritual. Beggars hold out withered hands as pilgrims with shaved heads hand out food to the poor. Two large, functional bridges cross the wide, straight river, which rushes grey and cold from the glacial melt of the Himalaya. All along the banks, as far as the eye can see, steps or *ghats* lead down to the river, where chain railings prevent people being swept away by the fast-flowing water; the *ghats* writhe with people, thousands of them undressing to bathe, while swimmers are whisked along by the fast current.

Bizarrely, the pageant atmosphere, the straight river and the crowds on the banks put me in mind of Henley, where I would go every July to watch my school compete in the Royal Regatta.

We crossed the bridge to the crowded old town, alongside troupes of Rajasthani farmers in turbans and bearded sadhus in orange robes. Walking up the river's right bank, opposite an enormous white statue of Shiva, we arrived at *Asthi Pravah Ghat*, where ashes are traditionally immersed. The *pandit*, dressed in white cotton, bade my sister and I to sit down, with barely an introduction and none of the pastoral care that one might expect from a priest. Before I knew what was happening, the ceremony had begun. Halfway through he even started haggling with my cousin over the price of his services.

As we poured the last of our dad's ashes into the river, a neighbouring priest argued about where exactly we should put them. It hardly felt like the intimate ritual for which I had waited so long and travelled so far. At the end of the 15-minute ceremony the priest disappeared, leaving me with a hollow disappointment in my stomach.

We wandered the back alleys of Haridwar, past cows and cafes, before finding our priest sitting on the floor in a small room with a curtain for a door. Inside were stacks of bound papers, one of which he had opened in front of him. The businesslike manner was gone; he had become far more amenable now that he had been paid.

He explained that the books were a history, with a recording of every single member of my family who had visited Haridwar: whenever a person died, his or her name was recorded in neat Sanskrit, and the family members who brought the ashes signed the page. Dad's name was duly recorded, as were the names of all of his brothers and all of their sons (as it is they who will carry on the family name), before the priest pointed out the signature of my grandfather and great-grandfather.

"This book," he began reverently, "contains your family records of thirteen generations, over five hundred years. And the rest of the books go back even further – over two thousand years." My sister and I carefully signed our names beneath the latest script, making us part of a living history that predates the Roman arrival in Britain.

Before we left, the *pandit* mentioned that this was an incredibly auspicious day to have done the *Tharpan*. Astrology is integral to Hinduism and, quite by accident, we had arrived on the day of a solar eclipse, so any rituals performed were extra-potent. "You couldn't have done a better job for your father," he assured me. "His soul will now be at peace, the restlessness that you have felt these last years will fade." And apparently I will have three sons.

In the days afterwards, my sister and I wound down from the intensity of our experience by visiting Rishikesh – once a popular destination on the Hippy Trail, thanks to a visit by four Liverpudlian musicians. The shore of the river is dotted with so many temples that I wondered how there could be enough pilgrims to go around, and with the Ganges languidly beginning its journey across the plains to Calcutta (Kolkata), it was everything I expected from mystical India.

In between white-water rafting and yoga, I felt the weight of six years falling off my shoulders. I had achieved everything I had set out to do, and more than fulfilled my duties. The rite of passage *had* taken me into a new stage of life: I felt a new and profound sense of comfort with my heritage; and I had finally completed that journey with Dad that had begun all that time and distance ago.

PIROGUE: DESCENT OF THE RIVER LULUA, DRC

Charlie Walker

For *Sidetracked* magazine
December 2014

The river had become too fast, and the rocks too many. We hadn't prepared for this; we hadn't had a chance to stop and scout ahead by foot. Having finally fought our way free of a narrow, overgrown channel of quick water running through dense forest, our lumbering pirogue (a traditional dugout canoe) suddenly surged into the open. Archie and I, already exhausted, looked ahead in panic.

We were speeding towards a churning field of rapids. Boulders littered the wide waterway, each threatening to undo us. We survived a couple of unplanned 360° pirouettes among obstacles and rogue currents before the breaks became too high and we inevitably struck a rock. Water gushed in and, desperately attempting to prevent the pirogue sinking, we leapt out. The fierce current hauled us over shallow rocks to the end of the rapids.

Our pirogue's nose had sunk, but the rear was held near the surface by the empty water containers we used as buoyancy aids. Bags floated off in various directions while we frantically thrashed back and forth in the still-speeding water, shepherding them back to the moving "base" of our sinking canoe.

In the thrall of the raging water, we guided the submerged pirogue to a thickly wooded bank. The sun was setting. I'd been wet for the last two hours and was shivering violently. We'd survived the rapids, but lost our map. From here on it would be an expedition into the unknown. We desperately needed to make a fire. Our situation looked bleak.

With all the dire warnings we'd received about how unfeasible it was to descend the river Lulua, it might have been hubris that made us try. Internet searches returned results which all contained the keyword "unnavigable". Countless villagers and rivermen warned us of crocodiles, hippos and rapids – lots of rapids; waterfalls even. But we were stubborn.

We'd hatched the plan to cross the Democratic Republic of the Congo (DRC) by bicycle and pirogue months earlier. Meticulous document forging for visas was followed by 1,000 miles of cycling and finally our arrival in Sandoa. This crumbling colonial town sits on the Lulua which carves a snaking route northwards, parallel to the nearby Angolan border, and spills into the Kasai which, in turn, feeds the mighty Congo.

An educational, but frustrating, week was spent cycling along sand footpaths through sedate forest villages, trying to persuade suspicious fishermen to sell us a pirogue. Each day the laid-back village men seemed only inclined to make a deal "keisho" (tomorrow). They all asked for just a few days to go fishing and thus earn enough money to cover the period necessary to have a new pirogue made. Yet, they never seemed to go fishing – things don't happen fast in the bedlam that is the Congo today.

We finally succeeded in obtaining a canoe for a wildly inflated price and set about patching holes in the 5.5-metre-long, 40-year-old craft. By the time we had finished, we were equipped with a low-sitting, hollowed-out tree trunk and a week of supplies. A crowd watched us shakily push off into the current one afternoon and carve the tentative first strokes of our voyage. We had no experience of rivers, let alone pirogues. This was reflected by the doubtful faces of the unusually quiet onlookers. Our river life – a steep, waterborne learning curve – had begun.

The days were largely routine unless rapids intervened, which they did increasingly often. The river slowly shed its dramatic shroud of mist each chilly morning, and we took turns as helmsman in the more comfortable rear seat. Lunches were bolted down whilst perched on the grand and twisting old tree roots that lined the bank, or taken on the water: one man eating, one steering. The

80-metre-wide river twisted and turned back on itself in tight bends reminiscent of those ubiquitous aerial shots of the snaking, jungle-pressed Amazon.

Towards the end of the second day we approached some islands. The current subtly quickened and, before we had time to do anything about it, we were committed to running a small set of rapids. The breakers were only about 30 cm high, but proved enough to lap generously over the sides near the stern and slowly start to sink us. Archie at "midship" had begun to jubilantly cheer that we'd come safely through, just as I shouted that we were going down. He looked shocked by this, and down we went.

After a few chaotic minutes, I managed to reach the bank with the rope and haul in the canoe, our sodden kit, and my bag-clutching partner. We bailed out the pirogue and busied ourselves with wood-collecting, fire-lighting and putting up drying lines. This rapid had been little more than a strong ripple. We'd have to be more prepared next time, because there would be more.

The men we met on the river (there were rarely any women, and those there were fled from us) enthusiastically gave us advice on the obstacles ahead and how best to approach them. However, estimates of distance could vary by hundreds of kilometres. Each knew their short stretch of river, but little beyond that. We rarely knew where we were or how far we'd travelled.

These kindly, self-sufficient people are so remote and unconnected from their fellow countrymen that war could easily come and go, sweeping through the region, without them ever knowing. There is no road access and the river's challenging nature leaves them extremely isolated. They spend their days smoking fish, or checking and setting fishing lines on trees overhanging the banks. Smaller fish are thrown into giant baskets woven from branches and suspended in the water. They are later scooped out when they've grown larger. The people eat almost exclusively fish and are consequently all under five foot tall.

When food ran short, Archie and I would land at one of the occasional places where large pirogues act as ferry crossings on the small tracks connecting villages. Whichever one of us forfeited a much-needed rest (by losing at rock paper scissors) would then cycle away from the water and inevitably end up being questioned by suspicious village elders who demanded papers, while a tight crowd of incredulous gawkers pressed ever closer. There was rarely anything other than cassava, fish and tropical fruit on sale. Our diet was therefore simple, but the daily exertion made each meal gratifying enough.

The journey became a balance of pleasant paddling on placid stretches of water, and fraught periods of activity when presented with rapids. We landed as soon as we thought white water might soon present itself, or we heard it, and scouted ahead on the banks. Most rapids consisted of multiple channels through rocks and islands. Choosing the right one was as essential as it was impossible.

Our two-man system of relaying the pirogue gradually through the rapids quickly developed and we became a smooth, cohesive team. We also improved at picking our way through less severe white water without disembarking. A vocabulary of curt, barked commands formed, and an effective system of simultaneous bailing out and steering was created.

Occasionally we enlisted the help of local men for a few dollars or some cigarettes. At one waterfall, a whole village helped us circumvent this major obstacle by dragging the pirogue a couple hundred metres over sun-blanched rock. My teeth were set on edge by the worrisome grating sound coming from the already battered underside of the hull.

Frequently, we darted down narrow side channels of water before daunting rapids in the hope of avoiding the worst of the danger. This strategy rarely bore fruit and we were usually dragged into fallen trees or hanging vines by the unrelenting current. Tight steering was difficult in our clumsy vessel and was not made easier by the jutting extremities of our bicycles stacked on its bow.

If we got caught up in branches, we had to jump in, grab hold of a branch or vine and start hacking away at it with a machete, taking care not to get swept away with the freshly liberated foliage. Drifting down one such channel, an unseen fish hook in a tree snagged on my matted hair and nearly plucked me off my perch in the stern.

In these instances, hopelessly lost down some unmapped jungle waterway, we were torn between exuberance at our intrepid adventure, fear of crocodiles, and dismay at the hazardous situation we'd rushed into. Nobody knew where we were. But that was, in part, why we were there.

The daily tonic to the exertion and anxiety of facing the unknown around each bend in the river was making camp. Each evening we'd nose into slack water among the trees, pitch tents and slump down by a campfire to cook and unwind. Often our camping spots were soothing, picturesque shelves of sandy ground perched just above the seasonally low water. They were enclosed by gnarled webs of trees and a labyrinthine spread of roots. Occasional visits from curious men were a refreshing opportunity to chat and meet Congolese under more relaxed circumstances than on the water.

After a particularly challenging gauntlet of rocks and raging water one evening, we approached a ring of huts with a smokestack perched high on a clear bank. We landed and began chatting to the bewildered small man we found there. M'baz welcomed us and we brewed three cups of sweet tea on his fire while he contentedly puffed on the cigarettes we'd produced.

M'baz showed us to one of the five huts and indicated that we should sleep there. The circular domed huts were two metres across and shoulder-high (for us) inside. They were made from dry grass hung over a wicker-woven frame. The doorway was a metre-high opening. In the morning, our host's companions – two smiling men with twists of muscle like tight metal cable – returned from their lines each bearing a fish almost a metre long with gills still gulping.

In time, we acclimatised to our otherwise alien environment. However, as our capabilities increased, our strength waned. Regular stumbling around on unseen jagged rocks in fast-flowing water soon meant our feet and shins were covered with cuts which were impossible to keep clean. Our hands spent too much time wet and with rough ropes running through them. We each owned a mess of torn knuckle caps and open, weeping wounds. Insect bites compounded things.

Besides the rapids, risks seemed to be accumulating. We began to hear hippos honking in the night and we passed a crowd of men celebrating their victory over a four-metre-long crocodile. In addition, a couple of cracks in the pirogue's prow were growing longer and wider day by day. We knew it was only a matter of time before the river either beat us or forced our surrender.

Until then we enjoyed the ride and wondered which outcome we'd prefer.

THE ANCIENT GAME THAT SAVED A VILLAGE

Jack Palfrey

For *BBC Travel*
May 2017

The green paint on the walls of Marottichal's village tea shop had started to flake, like coin scrapings on a scratch card, exposing a light blue tone of a bygone era. Perhaps this was once a rowdy bar or beer shop. But not anymore.

Mr Unnikrishnan, the tea shop's owner, sat opposite me at one of the wooden tables, his dark eyes fixated with an intimidating intensity on the chequered board that lay between us.

A callous hand rose and elegantly gripped the white bishop, sliding it gently into the black knight and toppling it over.

"He's got you now," said the spectating Baby John, slurping his chai to suppress a grin.

I surveyed the bleak scene unfolding before me. My few remaining pieces were backed into a corner, eager to surrender.

Around the tea shop's four other tables similar intense battles of wits were being fought, while a dust-coated Videocon television set languished on a shelf at the back of the room, unplugged and ignored.

Resorting to distraction, I poked a petrified pawn one square forward and asked Unnikrishnan why this game resonates so much with the people of Marottichal, a remote forest village in northern Kerala.

"Chess helps us overcome difficulties and sufferings," said Unnikrishnan, taking my queen. "On a chessboard you are fighting, as we are also fighting the hardships in our daily life."

With a feigned bravado I took one of Unnikrishnan's isolated pawns.

"And is it really that popular?" I asked.

Unnikrishnan shot me a wry smile. "Come, you can see for yourself," he said, rising from the table.

I looked down to find my king cowering, surrounded by a murderous mob of white plastic pieces.

I guessed that was checkmate.

It was mid-morning and Marottichal's tree-lined main street was busy, yet oddly quiet. The forest breeze didn't carry the vexatious shrill of traffic horns – the deafening symphony of most Indian towns – but instead silently stirred the strips of bright bunting zigzagging overhead.

The bus stop opposite Unnikrishnan's tea shop was full of people, but no one seemed to be going anywhere. Instead, the gathered crowd were squatted on their haunches, watching an intense chess match play out between two greying gentlemen. The men sat cross-legged and barefoot, their *lungis* (sarongs) taut across their thighs.

I soon spotted the bus a short distance away, though it carried no passengers; the engine was off, and the driver had turned from the wheel to contest a quick chess match with the conductor before the start of their next shift.

Friends on pavements, spouses on benches, colleagues over shop countertops; the black-and-white board perforated every scene. Around the corner from the tea shop on the veranda of Unnikrishnan's own home, reportedly one of the village's most popular gaming spots, no fewer than three matches were taking place.

"In other Indian villages perhaps the maximum number of people that know chess is less than fifty," said Baby John, president of the Chess Association of Marottichal. "Here four thousand of the six thousand population are playing chess, almost daily.

"And it is all thanks to this wonderful man," he added, gesturing to Unnikrishnan.

Fifty years ago, Marottichal was a very different place. Like many villages in northern Kerala, alcoholism and illicit gambling were rife among its small population. Having developed a zeal for chess while living in the nearby town of Kallur, Unnikrishnan moved back to his afflicted home town and opened his tea shop, where he began teaching customers to play chess as a healthier way to pass the time.

Miraculously, the game's popularity flourished while drinking and gambling declined. The village's enthusiasm for the ancient pastime, which is believed to have originated in India in the sixth century, has now become so great that Unnikrishnan estimates one person in every Marottichal household knows how to play.

"Luckily for us chess is more addictive than alcohol," Baby John said.

Not only did the archaic game scupper alcoholism and supersede clandestine card games, but it has engrained itself into Marottichal's identity, and, according to Baby John, it continues to protect the town's residents from modern pitfalls.

"Chess improves concentration, builds character and creates community," he said. "We don't watch television here; we play chess and talk to each other."

"Even the kids?" I asked.

Unnikrishnan shot me another wry smile.

It was lunchtime when we arrived at Marottichal Primary School, a cluster of blue walls and orange-tiled roofs, to find the dusty courtyard awash with frenzied children, like a startled flock of pigeons in a public square. But through the fray of bodies, I could see a row of children seated serenely at a line of tables.

We approached the nearest pair, who were perched at a discoloured bench with a chessboard between them. Vithun and Eldho, both 12 years old, sported matching tufts of black hair and shared a tangible enthusiasm for chess – with a fervid admiration for one piece in particular.

"The knight is the best," Vithun said.

"Definitely," Eldho replied.

"It's the most powerful."

"You can move it in any direction!"

In a country undergoing rapid digitalisation, fanning widespread fears about Indian youth becoming disconnected from their country and culture, it was strange to hear two children talk so enthusiastically about a 1,000-year-old board game that's interwoven into India's history. Surely they would prefer to be watching television, I wondered out loud.

"Chess is best!" shouted Eldho as he sprung from his seat, almost toppling the board. Vithum scowled at him.

"Last year we came to the school with fifteen chessboards and invited the children to learn chess," Baby John explained as we fought our way back through the courtyard. "The following week we went back and all the children in the classroom had bought chessboards of their own."

The positive response from the students, paired with their belief in the sanative qualities of the game, has led the Chess Association of Marottichal to request that the authorities include chess as part of the official school syllabus. This, they believe, will aid their vision of living in a village where everyone plays chess.

"Only then can we truly call ourselves a chess village," Baby John concluded, explaining that he believes the title will cement Marottichal's association to the much-loved sport and its edifying principles.

The wholesome lifestyle promoted by the village is seemingly attractive to Keralites, indicated by the remote area's growing population despite relatively high land prices. The village has also lured visitors from as far away as Germany and the US keen to learn the game or hone their skills.

But despite this, as we trudged back to the tea shop a lingering doubt gnawed at me: would a community centred on an ancient board game be able to withstand the rapid wave of modernisation sweeping across the Indian subcontinent?

My fears were heightened when we neared a group of teenagers tapping away on their smartphones, a sight that prompted me to voice these concerns to Unnikrishnan and Baby John.

But as we drew closer, the three of us could see what was commanding the group's undivided attention: they were all playing chess online.

Unnikrishnan gave me one last smile.

I guessed that was checkmate.

WET,
WET, WET

William Gray

For *Wanderlust*
June 2005

The squall rounded on us like a wet spaniel. In just a few exuberant seconds it drenched us with rain and whipped the sea into a frisky, unruly mood. Waves began to sluice over the bows of our sea kayaks, puddling in the neoprene spray skirts that clamped us to our cockpits like giant sink plungers. Ben White, our 21-year-old weather-resistant guide, peered happily from under a bright yellow sou'wester and delivered his meteorological verdict. "Looks like it's going to seriously crap out this afternoon," he shouted over the maelstrom of wind and spray.

Perhaps Captain James Cook had similar premonitions when he peered into this corner of New Zealand's Fiordland in 1770 and named it Doubtful Sound. The great mariner decided to give it a miss and continued his voyage along the west coast of South Island. However, had he sailed the *Endeavour* through the narrow entrance to this 40-km-long inlet he would have found himself in New Zealand's second-largest fiord and, at 421 m, its deepest. Today Doubtful Sound lies in the 21,000-sq-km Fiordland National Park, a majestic chunk of wilderness carved by glaciers and cloaked in ancient forest. When it comes to statistics, however, it is Fiordland's average rainfall that deluges the mind. Up to 8 metres of the stuff pelts the region every year – most of it falling, it seemed, during the two days I went kayaking in Doubtful Sound.

But don't let me put you off. Sea kayaking is, by its very nature, a damp undertaking. "Real kayakers don't mind getting their feet wet," Bill Gibson of Fiordland Wilderness Experiences told me earlier. I had nodded sagely. After all, by then I had already spent all of two mornings nurturing my kayaking skills at some of New Zealand's other renowned paddling spots.

The first was Otago Peninsula on South Island's east coast. The sea was so placid when guide Matt McFadyen and I launched our two-person kayak that we could hear the sighs of breath from a sea lion surfacing 200 metres away. Paddling out from the coastal hamlet of Portobello we were surrounded by white-fronted terns plunge-diving for fish, each splash carrying clearly, like pebbles tossed in a pond. "It doesn't get much better than this," said Matt as we settled into an easy rhythm, wavelets chuckling beneath our bows. "You get such a great perspective of marine life from a sea kayak."

He was right. Rounding Taiaroa Heads, we confronted a brisk south-westerly, strong enough for the albatrosses that nest on the clifftop above to get airbourne. As they soared overhead, cradling the wind on 3-m wingspans, fur seals cavorted amongst writhing arms of honey-coloured kelp or preened their glistening pelts on rocky haul-outs. Stewart Island shags streamed from their nests like the opening salvo of arrows in a medieval battle, while yellow-eyed penguins huddled nearby.

If anything, my second kayaking trip put me on even more intimate terms with New Zealand's wild outdoors. The Southern Alps might not strike you as much of a kayaking destination, however a small iceberg-strewn lake at the snout of Mueller Glacier near Mt Cook proved an exhilarating setting for a morning's paddle.

"High fun, low stress." That was the philosophy of my guide, Chance, as we nosed about the glacial tarn, weaving between icebergs that varied from gravel-encrusted hulks to delicate sculptures of gas-flame blue. Hemmed in by Mt Sealy on one side and the ice-fluted cone of 3,754-m Mt Cook on the other, we paddled in reverent silence, pausing occasionally to pluck small chunks of pure ice to suck on.

With two such inspiring trips under my spray skirt you can appreciate why sea kayaking was becoming my obsession. As I travelled south towards Fiordland the opportunity to join a paddling expedition in one of the southern hemisphere's great wilderness areas was irresistible.

Right from the start, however, my two-day adventure on Doubtful Sound struck me as a far more serious undertaking. For a start it would take three hours simply to reach our launch point at Deep Cove – crossing Lake Manapouri by water taxi before taking a 4WD vehicle across Wilmot Pass. Then there would be the unpleasant locals to contend with. "Your sandflies are gathering," Bill Gibson told us at the pre-departure briefing in Te Anau. "They know you're coming and they're looking forward to joining you in your kayaks."

At 6 a.m. the following morning our group of eight had dwindled to six – not because of the bloodsucking promise of sandflies, but the fact that gale-force winds, born and bred in the Southern Ocean, were hurling themselves at Fiordland. So much rain had fallen overnight that Te Anau's famous glow-worm caves were inaccessible and the road to Milford Sound had been closed due to flooding.

"Rain in Fiordland is spectacular," said our ever-optimistic guide, Ben White. "Nowhere does waterfalls like we do." And so it was with a mixture of trepidation and anticipation that our depleted party ventured west towards Doubtful Sound.

The wind had eased, but it was still raining when we reached Deep Cove. A nearby waterfall beat its steady, ominous thunder, sheets of spray spurting like high-pressure steam where the cascade struck the surface of the fiord. I traced the gushing plume of water upwards for 500 m, perhaps more, before it was snuffed out by clouds slumped on Doubtful Sound's forest-clad cliffs. Looking west, sea, mountain and cloud merged into an ethereal, monotone landscape, like a watercolour painting that had a life of its own, constantly evolving at the whim of rain, light and wind.

The effect was mesmerising, soporific – but not for long. Ben had a reality check for us. From two large holdalls he pulled a worrying amount of clothing that was to be our kayaking garb. First on was a lightweight base layer, followed by a 5-mm-thick long-john wetsuit and fleece jumper. Next came the spray skirt, hoisted to armpit level. Over this went a waterproof paddling jacket, leaving just a woollen hat and Paddington Bear-style sou'wester – the latter designed to prevent rainwater trickling down the back of your neck.

Having cajoled ourselves into these outfits (twice if you'd forgotten to visit the toilet beforehand), Ben gave us a safety briefing. Capsize drill looked so easy with the kayaks hauled, high and dry, on a pebbly beach. "Your spray skirt is like an ejector seat," Ben said. "Just pull this tag at the front and you'll pop out and float to the surface." And then what, I was wondering, but Ben was already explaining that our kayaks were the best money could buy; none were more stable or buoyant. And with that, we gathered our resolve and our paddles, launched the kayaks and started paddling.

Even with all our camping gear, food and spare clothing stowed away, the sea kayaks were remarkably easy to paddle and manoeuvre. Sitting in the stern cockpit, Rhalena, a photographer from Los Angeles, soon mastered the rudder controls and concentrated instead on plying me with chocolate chip cookies, convinced that I needed the energy. In fact, we were only going to paddle for five hours that first day, covering around 15 km. It sounds a lot, but sea kayaking is more about slow exploration, nosing about inlets, drifting with the current and "rafting up" for a chat with other kayakers, rather than hell-bent blazing paddles.

Hugging the shoreline we made our way into Hall Arm, one of the narrow, fingerlike branches of Doubtful Sound. Never before had I seen, or heard, water in so many guises. From the constant rumble of cataracts and patter of droplets from saturated moss to the hiss of rain and rhythmic swish of our paddles, water permeated my senses. But just when I thought it would also seep through my multilayered clothing, the rain stopped. Clouds began to fracture overhead, a stubborn scrap snagging on 1,509-m Mt Danae like sheep's wool on a barbed wire fence. Sunlight bloomed amongst the thick tangle of beech trees that crowded the shoreline, backlighting shaggy growths of moss and lichen that festooned their twisted branches.

Elsewhere, bare granite gleamed like slivers of bone through the verdant flesh of the forest. These great scars, Ben told us, were created by "tree avalanches" where the thin layer of rich humus covering the precipitous cliff faces suddenly gave way, sending huge swathes of forest crashing into the fiord. Tannins leached from the decaying vegetation tainted the water a shade of well-brewed tea. "So much rain falls here," Ben went on, "that it creates a permanent layer of freshwater." To demonstrate his point, he scooped up a handful to drink.

There was no shortage of freshwater on land when we pulled into a tiny rocky beach for lunch. The rain had restarted and, despite Ben's best efforts to rig a tarpaulin shelter, we were soon soaked. Worse still were the sandflies. Making up for their curious absence at Deep Cove, the tiny, winged menaces soon had us slapping ourselves like a troop of Tyrolean dancers. They were especially partial to ankles, eyelids and the soft bits behind your ears.

According to Māori legend, Fiordland was carved by the god, Tuterakiwhanoa. But when the goddess of the underworld,

Hinenuitepo, saw how beautiful it was she was concerned that people would want to live there forever, so she decided to send the sandfly to remind them of their mortality and frailty. Bless her. How thoughtful.

We took some consolation from the fact that only the female sandfly is a nipper (apparently she needs a blood meal before laying eggs). Nevertheless, it was a relief to get back on the water where Hinenuitepo's legacy was far less of a nuisance. A brief sighting of a pair of rare crested penguins proved a pleasant distraction and then our minds were focused on the logistics of spending a night under canvas.

Beaching the kayaks on a spit of land that jutted into Hall Arm, Ben led us into a patch of podocarp forest – a strange, twilight world of shrubs and tree ferns pierced by the tall, straight trunks of hardwood giants like the rimu and totara. Strung across a raised deck in a small clearing was an insect-proof shelter, from which a narrow path meandered through the dripping forest to a few root-free patches where we could pitch our tents.

By dusk, we had hauled the kayaks well above the high tide mark, erected our tents and changed into dry clothes. Huddled in the communual insect shelter we then set about our next wilderness challenge: dinner. I was quietly pleased with my culinary effort of pre-cooked rice and tinned pasta sauce with slices of ham (left over from lunch) cunningly added at the last minute. Then I noticed that some of the others had brought fresh Parmesan cheese with them and were grating it onto spectacular creations of spaghetti bolognaise accompanied by red wine and a fresh side salad.

Ben didn't seem hungry. Instead he dished out some serious food for thought. He had just received the following day's weather forecast on his satellite phone. A new low was heading our way;

temperatures were expected to plummet; there would be strong winds and, of course, rain. Plenty of it.

There was a lull before the storm struck — a strained period of calm when the plaintive high-pitched cries of kiwis echoed through the forest. We emerged from our tents before dawn. During the night a tree had fallen near camp, waking us with a jolt and leaving us wide-eyed and twitchy.

Reluctantly, we stripped from our warm, dry camp clothes and braced ourselves for the sodden paddling attire that had been festering overnight in the kayaks. I will never forget the sensation of putting on that wetsuit. It was like slipping into the skin of a long-dead seal.

We repacked the kayaks and paddled furiously, desperate for the exercise to warm our cold, stiff muscles. There was fresh snow on the surrounding peaks and the sky looked bruised and sullen. "Remember to keep your bows into the wind," Ben shouted. And then the squall bore down on us. Drawing a grey veil across the Sound it machine-gunned rain in our faces and swatted our paddles.

For a moment we were caught broadside, the kayak rolling dangerously on its beam. Thrusting our paddles out like the stabilisers on an outrigger canoe, Rhalena and I braced ourselves for a dunking. But somehow the kayak kept upright. Surfing on waves we made for the lee of Elizabeth Island where the others were already waiting, flushed with adrenaline.

We beached on Elizabeth Island to heat some water for coffee. Clutching mugs and stamping our feet to combat the cold, we stared at the billycan waiting for the water to boil. Richard Henry wasn't exaggerating when, in 1896, he claimed, "This is fine country for the waterproof explorer." But at that moment, we were far from waterproof. In fact, we were very wet and very cold. Ben must have read our minds. Grabbing the billycan, he poured the lukewarm contents over our numb feet. Never had water looked or felt so good. And, what's more, I was now a real kayaker. I had got my feet well and truly wet.

FOOTPRINTS

Tim Hannigan

For *The Clearing*
August 2018

I thought at first that they were some kind of strange house brick, paper-white in the thinning light, scattered across the track with the new grass coming through. But the sound they made caused me to pause: a glassy tinkle under my boot heels. I looked back uncertainly towards the gimcrack farmyard where I had left the car, then squatted down. A mass of them: uneven lozenges, perfectly flat on one side, cleanly curved on the other. The edges of the pile had been ground to chalk under the wheels of a passing tractor, but those at the centre were intact, cool and hard to the touch. I lifted one, and saw the letters, scratched into the flatter surface: Indira A. Then other names came clear across the pile: Ms G Wilson; Mr Goswami; Sarah S.

A small lurch of horror: I was holding a plaster cast of a human foot.

Hundreds of them, each marked with the name of its owner. What were they doing here, things of such intimacy, dumped in a farm track beyond the brink of the city? I fought the urge to recoil and fling the cast that I held aside. I replaced it as gently as I could, and stepped away, unpleasant electricity prickling up my forearms and across my scalp. It felt like a moment from another land; a discovery in the flayed fields of a country a few seasons beyond evil. But these were only plaster casts, and this was only Leicestershire.

I moved away uneasily, the motorway roaring to the right like a wind-wrecked groundswell.

I had sat in my car with a bare hour of daylight to spare, the map unfolded over the steering wheel. Three days of sudden heat in mid-April, and the city had gone into a strange convulsion, dotting the park beside the university with pallid, cross-legged figures, mobile phones cradled like alms bowls. It made me suddenly and overwhelmingly claustrophobic, aching for home ground where the moors would all be in a turmeric blaze of gorse.

I scanned the map for a right of way, the nearest green stitch through the fields, and found it, just above the blue right angle of a motorway junction. It was maybe two miles from where I sat. Better yet: there was a way through; a C-road that bled from urban orange to rural yellow as it passed beneath the motorway; a forgotten weakness in the city's defences.

I folded the map, started the engine, and swung out into the traffic.

———————————

Beyond the plaster casts, the path crossed a brook and rose to the edge of a rape field. The ground here was wet, yielding beneath my boots and marked by no footprints but my own. No one had walked this way for weeks, maybe since before the winter. The motorway roared to the right, and the path ran in beside it, though the cars were invisible, 20 feet below. A magpie angled up ahead, then dropped into a hedge like a paper plane, cackling furiously at my intrusion.

I was still unnerved by the plaster feet, and all of this was very strange. To the left was a long spinney like the back of a mastodon, the falling sun just snagged on its upper edge. To the right, across the evening flood tide of traffic, were pavements still throbbing faintly with the heat of the day. A quarter-mile ahead a red-and-white postage stamp rose above the thorns: Colonel Sanders, flying over the Leicester Forest East Services.

And then suddenly stranger still: OS sheet 233 abruptly peeled away from the ground reality: a new road, cutting through the fields towards some satellite suburb where the map showed only a path. I climbed over the fence and wandered along the freshly seeded verge. A rough mound of earth rose on one side, and a skeletal trio reared into view at its summit: three boys on scramblers, set against the coppery wash of the western sky. They looked down at me for a moment, helmeted heads mantis-like, then vanished into the country with a triple snarl. I expected to see them again, trailing dust along a field edge when I cut back south, away from the new road, but there was nothing.

Another spinney here, the branches still thin with winter and the fading light coming through in bars. The tops were lousy with wood pigeons. They shifted at my passing, wings clattering, and I drew a peristaltic pulse of movement above me as I walked the length of the wood.

There were three more of these spinneys in view: square blocks, two or three acres apiece, separated by half-mile stretches of pasture. This pattern was no accident. They were old fox coverts, and when I paused and unfolded the map I could see that there were still others, east of the motorway, fixed as if in amber amongst the suburbs. Once – probably within living memory – packs of strange hounds had clamoured through their undergrowth on winter Saturdays while cavalcades of top-hatted gentry waited on horseback in the flanking fields.

The coverts now fossilised within the city still had their names on the map: Meynell's Gorse; Foxholes Spinney; the Osiers. Those outside the motorway were nothing but green blocks in the white fields. But they *would* have had names. To the west a reddish smudge showed a tractor, harrowing a field in the day's end. Someone out there probably still knew what these little woods were called, if only you knew where to ask.

In a gateway at the end of the spinney, a moment of sudden squalor: plywood and broken pallets; a yellow sand sack, marked with the phone number of a builders' merchant; a pane of glass, and an upended toilet. I didn't understand what had happened here. There are often squalid moments in farmland; broken concrete and feed sacks shunted into far corners, half-covered with boulders cleared from the fields. But this deposit – like the plaster feet – was something else, something inexplicable, something faintly uncanny.

At home I might have known already whose land this was. If not, I could have asked: *who's got the fields up by… up by…* But the woods were nameless on the map.

The line of the path dropped down a slight slope to the lane that led back to the farmyard where I had parked. Here another heap of junk, plasterboard and tiles.

Suddenly I understood. I was not the only person to have found this lane, this secret portal that took you out along the last street of pavement-mounted cars, and into the countryside. All the less reputable builders of the city knew it was here too, and at night their vans slipped out this way, hauled up on the green littoral like egg-laying turtles, and dropped their loads. Some, compelled by a strange discretion, turned through open gateways to leave their excretions away from the lane. And once – sometime last year perhaps – one of their number had carried a macabre cargo, the contents of an old storeroom from a chiropodist's clinic undergoing renovation, and dumped it in the first trackway so that the smooth imprints of people who might never walk this way now lay amongst the fields.

I walked back east along the lane. The flanking trees were full of bird noise and the ditch was foul with builders' waste. I paused at a gateway, and spotted a hare, loping purposefully down the slope towards me like a departing miscreant. I froze, and she kept coming. She was very close before she paused, recognising something out of place. But in this country strangely coloured deposits appeared nightly in the gateways, and after a moment she moved on forward, hesitantly now, folding and refolding her long body like the running gear of a steam train slowing towards a station. I stopped breathing, and she was a bare 20 feet away before finally she halted.

I could see the small pulses around her muzzle as she groped at the evening air for a signal, and I caught a brief intimation of a process coming to fulfilment, through the dusk darkly. She whipped around and bolted back the way she had come, throwing a triple volley of jinks into her course as if I might be powering after her like a lurcher, then was gone over the rise.

I walked on with a faint tremor in my fingertips.

It was very nearly dark when I got back to the car, parked in the sprouting nettles beside the barns. I stood in the lane. Ahead I could see the modest collection of high buildings in the city centre. Behind, the way I had come, the lane faded between fields and spinneys.

Many people would call the country through which I had walked a "liminal space". But no; this was a *place*. This was absolutely the countryside. The spinneys and fields had names, even if no mapmaker had ever thought to seek them out. If there was a limen it was the motorway itself. This farm, and the others around it, had watched the open ground between the fox coverts fill up, and the calcification creep towards them out of the east, until, in the late 1960s, they threw up the M1 like a dyke and the advance stopped. The nightly deposits in the gateways blew across like spindrift from a blood-dark sea.

I stood there for a long time, looking up and down the lane in both directions, and then, just as I was about to break myself away, the tractor I had seen in the distance earlier loomed suddenly out of the remembered country to the west. There was still a glow in the sky beyond, and the figure in the cab was backlit and broad, swaying with the easy bounce of the suspension. I stepped aside and raised a hand in greeting, and a hand went up in return – the familiar loose salute of a man in charge of a big machine. He swung right into a rutted trackway and rumbled off into other fields.

Down by the brook the plaster feet were white like bones in the gloaming.

TRAILING THE SNOW LEOPARD IN MOUNTAINOUS LADAKH

Lizzie Pook

For *The Evening Standard*
January 2020

"Shanku! Shanku!" The call comes at breakfast amid a sharp clatter of cutlery. I hurl my fork towards the table, scrambled eggs flying, and bolt for the door.

Outside, snow-bloated clouds mottle the sky, the air is knife-cold – chill enough to make your joints ache – and I raise my binoculars with shaking hands. Two creatures are picking their way across the mountainside. My shoulders drop slightly – it's wolves. They trot nimbly past some fluttering prayer flags, their bellies swollen from a recent feast.

It's an incredible sighting, but wolves are not why I am here. They are not why I've travelled to India's farthest reaches, through militarised towns and mountains, to the remote foothills of the mighty Himalayas.

Because this is the land of the snow leopard. The tiny village of Ulley in West Ladakh is surrounded by mountains whose crags shelter these magnificent big cats. Here, a small clutch of houses teeters at a breathtaking 14,000 feet.

Temperatures can plummet to minus 30°C in winter and the air is thin and flighty, getting away from you when your lungs need it most. I'm holed up at The Snow Leopard Lodge, a homestay run by Tchewang Norbu, a local man with an almost superhuman ability to seek out the rare animals. The lodge is a vital means of employment for locals and keen-eyed villagers work as "spotters", scouring the ice-ravaged landscape for a flash of fur or the coil of a heavy tail.

Snow leopards have a colossal range covering almost two million square kilometres in Central Asia. With only an estimated 4,080 to 6,500 in the wild, unsurprisingly, seeing them is a struggle. "Needle in a haystack" doesn't cover it. These are precipitous and hostile mountains, with incalculable nooks and crannies, towering granite boulders and unreachable valleys. But take a walk and you'll know that "Shan" is watching you. You'll feel it in your blood. You may even see signs. Scratch marks, faeces or pug marks in the dirt.

And so we spend our days being "watched" by snow leopards. We peer through our scopes, scour every rocky inch until our eyes ache, and hike sweeping, snow-dusted valleys. We see golden eagles being mobbed by alpine choughs. We spot impressive mountain goats silhouetted against the sky like helmeted Vikings. But we see no leopards. At night we watch wildlife documentaries or trawl through old camera trap footage of puffy-furred leopards. We fear that a TV screen is the closest we'll get to the "grey mountain ghost".

The final morning dawns with the scent of mountain lavender in the air. We head out for a short hike, feverishly raking the mountains for any final signs of life. No joy. Back at the lodge, some of the group rest in their rooms, but I walk up to the spotters' point to scan with them for a while.

Up here, the landscape is as still as a stopped clock. Then, quick as a pistol crack, spotter Namgyal begins to shout: "Shan! Shan! Shan!" His eyes are urgent, his words sitting in the air like smoke. Norbu rushes over, checks the scope, and turns to me, laughter lines etched into his face. My heart gallops. I put my eye to the glass. It's there all right. On the far ridge. Silhouetted like a sphinx – the unmistakable shape of a snow leopard. I shriek. The leopard hauls itself to its feet, tail as fat as a python that's just eaten. Suddenly, something else totters into view. The breath snags in my throat. It's a cub. No, two cubs. I blink cartoonishly as they clamber onto their mother's back, leaping from rock to rock like aerialists. There are no guarantees in these mountains but to witness these creatures, hardy animals that are the embodiment of what is wild and unreachable, is to really feel like you've seen a ghost.

THE HOTHOUSE HEART OF THE JUNGLE

Adrian Phillips

For *National Geographic Traveller*
November 2017

Stepping into Yasuni National Park isn't a toe-dip into wilderness. It's a full-on dive into the rainforest, where the air is heavy with the scent of wet leaves, and the darkness of night tightens around you like the coils of a python...

THE JUNGLE AT NIGHT

"What the Christ is that?!" comes the cry from the compost toilet, before David makes a flapping exit through the blue sheet that serves for a door. Fredy interrupts what he's doing – namely, evicting a swarm of ants from my rucksack – to offer his expert opinion. "Wolf spider," he informs us, as we peer around the curtain at the hairy creature squatting robustly on the wooden seat. I've barely time to worry whether the wolf spider is so-called because it's the size of a wolf or because it hangs around in packs, when our attention is diverted once more. "Erm, Fredy?" calls Nick, his voice a touch brittle. "Could I borrow you? There's a scorpion on my tent."

Our camp for the night is basic: four small bell tents, a bucket shower behind a makeshift screen of woven leaves, and a hole-in-the-ground loo (currently occupied). We've only been here an hour, and already Ecuador's rainforest has laid down some markers, dispatched a few scuttling scouts to dismantle our comfort zone and shake us free of any complacency. Wonder at me, it seems to say, but don't let down your guard. This isn't a toe-dip into wilderness before retreat to the downy pillows of a luxury lodge. We're staying right in the prickly, hothouse heart of the jungle, and as dusk falls its darkness tightens slowly round us like the coils of a python.

Having de-anted my bag and de-scorpioned Nick's tent, Fredy wants to show us what else is out in the night, and so we line up behind him and thread our way through the foliage. "Don't touch anything!" Fredy warns, but it's hopeless because the jungle is intent on patting me down. A creeper's tendril caresses my shoulder, a web catches my hair; moths buffet my eyebrows as they fuss about the head torch.

The mew of a black banded owl cleaves the air, which is humid, and heavy with the scent of wet leaves and the sound of cicadas. Cameo after cameo of jungle existence is captured in the white disc of Fredy's spotlight. A black-headed spider gorges on something with lacy wings, while a poisonous banana spider sits waiting in its web. We limbo beneath a striped caterpillar hanging from the leaves – "Be careful, its hairs can infect your skin!" – and watch a fishing spider lurking above a stream, biding its time. Somewhere a tree frog makes a quacking noise, like a dog toy being chewed.

Scorpion spider. Tawny-bellied screech owl. Diablo grasshopper, with the devil's face on it. In this real-life Gothic drama, the characters even have names of the night, and everything that moves against the forest's blackened backdrop seems to play the part of either the hunter or the hunted. What's increasingly unclear is which of the roles we are filling – whether we're stalking nature or nature's stalking us – and it's while I ponder this blurred line that a flurry of jagged wings fills my torchlight and bursts past my ear, sending me flailing and ducking to the ground. "False vampire bat," says an amused Fredy as I straighten up and fight to calm my breath. "It only eats fruit."

THE JUNGLE EXPERIENCE

This is the Mandari Panga Jungle Experience, a new tourism project set up by Fredy and his wife in the pristine rainforest of Yasuni National Park. It involves many of the local Mandari Panga community – a 150-strong group of indigenous Quichua people – in varying roles, with some employed as guides, others providing food. Most live several kilometres west of here, but one family is nearby, and before retiring to our tents in the undergrowth we'll cross the river to join them for a meal of chicken and rice, and to have our faces painted in the ceremonial patterns of a hunter (me), a fisherman (David) and – after earnest assurances it's a genuine job in these parts – a jungle man (Nick). Tomorrow we'll travel eastward along the River Tiputini, deeper and deeper into the rainforest, and further and further from any other souls.

For tourists, the project offers a rare taste of the Amazon at its remotest, but for Fredy it offers nothing less than the hope of salvation. Forget the army of predators prowling around them; the real threat to this fragile community lies beneath. Oil. The prospectors started circling Ecuador in the 1960s, persuading villages to sell drilling rights, and the pipeline is ever-present beside the road on the journey here from Quito, writhing through the landscape like a rust-brown anaconda. We'd passed an oil town shortly before reaching the national park, its greenery cleared for access roads, its people looking somehow hard-faced and hollow-eyed. At the foot of four roaring gas flares, the bodies of burnt insects formed mounds a metre high. The Mandari Panga community have so far resisted the oil dollars. But for how much longer? Fredy knows tourism can provide an alternative future. "We've something special here," he says simply.

OUT ON THE RIVER

That special something unfurls before us early the following day. After a candlelit breakfast of fried eggs and mashed plantain, we clamber unsteadily into dugout canoes. I join Nick, a writer from Northumberland, in one of the cedar-wood boats; Fredy steps sure-footed as a cat into the stern. David, an American who came to Quito 15 years ago and is founder of local tour operator Eos Ecuador, takes the other boat with a guide called Julio. "That's best for you guys – I seem to attract the bugs," David comments ruefully.

It's 5.45 a.m., a hinterland time, no longer night but not quite morning either. The air is washed with a sunless light, and mist rests like a sagging net on the crown of the forest. Julio and Fredy paddle stealthily, loose-limbed, each taking a few gentle strokes on one side before flicking the oar up and over his head in an elegant arc to take a few strokes on the other. The river oozes, flat and dense and silent. Alongside us the rainforest is immense and stock-still, not a leaf trembling, the trees silhouetted flat against the grey. I'm struck by a sense of the theatrical, of a stage set ready for the play of life.

And as we wait, the orchestra builds the atmosphere. Cicadas lay down the bassline with their enduring electric hum. Next, a woodpecker taps out a tempo, supported by a dove that repeats its single note, luxurious, haunting, and as regular as a metronome. On top of this comes the melody, piping whistles and echoing chimes, a huffy burst like someone working a bicycle pump, the ratcheting noise of a clock being wound, the bubbling of a cuckoo, its call like boiling water, and the sound of the oropendola, like a pebble dropped in a pool of liquid gold.

With a sort of guttural drum roll, the first members of the cast enter stage left. "Howler monkeys!" Fredy says, pointing to four red-furred figures emerging from the dry-ice haze at the top of a fig tree. "The males growl like that to mark their territory." We drift on, and birds start coming thick and fast. A pair of blue-headed parrots make a dash overhead, strangely front-heavy with their stunted tails, and protesting loudly about some outrage or other. We look in on an animated debate between cobalt-winged parakeets, who squawk back and forth among the acacia branches. An aloof, Guinness-beaked toucan stares into the distance, pretending not to hear.

Fredy and Julio direct the action, moving our gaze from one scene to the next. My eyes ache – genuinely ache! – from the effort of picking shapes from the knotted jumble of green and brown. "Spider monkey," they say, and I look straight at it but see nothing until the animal scratches a leg and reveals itself, as though spirited there by magic. Golden mantled tamarind monkeys walk head first down a trunk, white markings around their mouths like a toddler's milk moustache. Julio makes a chesty hissing noise at them, and they make a chesty hissing noise back.

We pass a snakebird on a log, red-capped cardinals on a twig, and then – at some hidden cue – the star turns appear, breaking along the bank with a clatter of slapping paws and splashing their way into the water. Three giant river otters, adults and a juvenile, beautiful animals but slightly eerie too, with something of the pit bull about their snouts and the reptile in their eyes. They rest chins on the surface, tracking us unblinkingly, and once more I'm conscious of roles reversed as the watchers become the watched.

ANACONDA LAGOON

By 10 a.m. the mist has turned to wispy cloud and the heat of the sun is at our necks. Nick and I enjoy the sight of a huge owl-eyed butterfly lolloping in front of our boat, and of David battling to free himself from a persistent bee that has buzzed around him for the last ten minutes. "I should give it a name," he calls across to us, swatting at his hair, and we nod sympathetically and try to keep straight faces. But shortly afterwards the atmosphere tautens as we pull into a channel where the sun can't follow, and Julio helps us out of the boats and into a swamp.

Places don't get more primeval and preying than this. The ground tries to fold us into itself, mud sucking as high as the middle of our thighs as we walk jerkily like robots and fight to hold on to our boots. Finally, thankfully, we find relief in a track of sorts. Julio moves lithely ahead of us, hacking with his machete. "Mind these," Fredy says protectively, stepping high-kneed over a bobbing line of leafcutter ants. "They can carry their leaves four kilometres," he adds with evident fondness. (Later I'll reflect on the lottery of life as Fredy eats lemon ants by the dozen off a coffee tree. "They taste great if you're thirsty!")

Anaconda Lagoon greets us with the eggy stink of decay. It's a black-water ecosystem very different from the Tiputini River, and a further reminder of Yasuni's biodiversity. The national park is a UNESCO World Biosphere Reserve, its 1.2 million acres making room for everything from giant kapok trees with crowns like mushroom clouds to ants tiny enough to hitchhike on the leaves carried by the leafcutter ants we've just left behind. Not far to the south of us is the Intangible Zone, an area home to two 'uncontacted' tribes who hunt with spears and blowpipes, and live in total isolation from the outside world. This had seemed extraordinary when considered in advance, but out on this festering oxbow lake I could easily believe we're the only people on earth.

We've joined another dugout, Fredy standing at the front, the better to scan the ragged vegetation spilling over the lake's edges. The water is inky and smooth, but occasionally it pulses as something invisible moves beneath like a muscle under skin. "I don't recommend swimming here," says Fredy quietly, and entirely unnecessarily. "There are big electric eels that can give you a shock of six hundred volts."

And, as the lake's name suggests, there are anacondas too, which like to bask on logs. For once, though, Fredy's radar is off beam. Instead, he finds a blood-red bird-eating snake, swirling shoals of tadpoles, a row of roosting long-nosed bats. A ribbed nest of warrior wasps, which, when we clap our hands, vibrates to a sound like marching soldiers – *pherlunk, pherlunk, pherlunk* – as thousands of wings beat a warning from within. Julio trails a fishing line, and pulls in a piranha with a hunched back and jagged underbite. But no anacondas.

"Last week, I saw one here seven metres long!" Fredy says, frustrated. "An anaconda will hypnotise you if you look it in the eye," he adds, and I keep my head fixed firmly forward until we're safely out of the lagoon.

FOREST MAGIC

Scientists will tell you it's a myth, of course, and that a snake is no more capable of hypnosis than it is of persuading Eve to eat an apple. But the jungle isn't a place of science, whatever the textbooks say. It's a place of potions and dream prophecies and tales passed from parent to child, an other-worldly kingdom where different laws apply. Nature's power can be something to fear, like the danger in the anaconda's eye. It can be something to harness: those white onions growing by the side of the path are used to treat burns, Julio says; the juice from this mushroom stalk can heal ear infections; these berries rubbed around a baby's head will cure its fever. It can even be downright bizarre. "Don't stare at that bird or your pants will break," Fredy cautions as we look up at a swallow-tailed kite.

That evening, Fredy reveals he's the son of a *yachak* – a wise man. We're sitting cross-legged in a circle on the floor, shelling cocoa beans still hot from roasting in the fire. "My father speaks with spirits of the forest and rivers, and guards people from bad energies," he says, and we just nod, unsurprised, and ask some practical questions – how long do his ceremonies last? How do the spirits communicate? – because out here it seems entirely plausible that things might be plucked from thin air.

When it comes to food, there's no greater magician than Alicia, Fredy's smiley mother-in-law. It's her stilted house we're in now, the sides open to the forest, and we'll spend our remaining nights in tents on thatched platforms Fredy has built a few metres away overlooking the river. While we work at the cocoa beans, Alicia chews on boiled *chontaduros*, spitting pieces of the orange palm fruit into a wooden bowl, and mashing them with a pestle. She's making *chicha*, a mildly alcoholic drink. "Chewing makes the *chicha* less slimy," Fredy explains.

Alicia helps us to grind cocoa beans and sugar into a glossy paste, from which she concocts a frothy hot chocolate, the sweetest of endings to a meal of Julio's piranha, served on banana leaves with local avocado and tomatoes. UNESCO has recognised Alicia's work in preserving traditional Amazonian cuisine. She teaches the village schoolchildren ancestral recipes, how to make chocolate and grow their own food sustainably. These are key lessons for the community to learn if the Mandari Panga project is to succeed. "So many lodges in Ecuador bring all their food in from Quito. We want to do things differently," Fredy says, rapping his knuckles on the floor.

CAN PIGS FLY?

It's the following morning, and we're halfway up a tree, hiding from wild pigs. White-lipped peccaries, to be exact, a hairy species that can weigh up to 100 lbs. We can't see the peccaries, but they're close, hundreds of them, their fusty scent on the leaves, their prints in the earth; bruised fruit skins litter the ground. The grunts of so many truffling snouts creates a low vibration through the forest, a sound almost man-made, like the thrum of a generator.

Peccary herds of this size are dangerous. The males can be aggressive, and if the group panics it will stampede blindly, flattening anything in its way. Julio had sensed them first as we walked the trail, putting a finger to his lips with an urgency I'd not seen before, the stakes raised in the turn of a moment. Fredy ushered us to a fallen tree, propped against another at 45 degrees, and we'd shuffled awkwardly up the trunk as high as we dared. Satisfied we're safely stored, Julio and Fredy remove their T-shirts to ensure they're better camouflaged, and melt away to scout the situation.

Straddling this tree is the very definition of a stress position. My thighs cramp, ants bite, and a twig keeps steady pressure on a part of me that shouldn't be pressured. Whenever Nick adjusts himself above, I receive a shower of bark and lichen. Fifteen minutes pass, then twenty. The thrumming rises and falls as the herd moves, sometimes close, sometimes further away. All we can do is wait.

From here, wrapped in its spiky embrace, corralled by its barrelling foot soldiers, the rainforest seems invincible. On the river, it had felt infinite, the trees at the bank just the frontline in an organic mass that stretched back forever. It's difficult to believe that this mass is a sum of parts, that its things can be counted, that at this moment there is a precise number of howler monkeys, of tarantulas, of white-eyed parakeets. That somewhere the uncontacted tribespeople can hear the same rumble of thunder as I can, and that their population can be tallied. That if you lose a tree, that's one lost from the total. That the jungle is half the size it was before the oil companies arrived.

Thirty minutes pass; there are squeals and a clacking of teeth. Another roll of thunder, the longest I've ever heard, and above us the canopy crackles with rain. All we can do is wait. For all its sorcery and stagecraft, the rainforest is powerless against the anaconda pipeline. This is a modern threat that requires a human solution, and Fredy's family are training guides and teaching the community about tourism, preparing their forest guardians. Every villager recruited is one added to the total.

"These are good people," Fredy had said. "I'm desperate to make this project succeed." Only time will tell if Fredy can work his magic. All we can do is wait. Meanwhile, I'll cling to this tree, push Nick's boot off my head, and cross fingers the pigs here can't fly.

PANTELLERIA, ITALY'S ELEMENTAL ISLAND

Antonia Quirke

For *Condé Nast Traveller*
April 2018

Jagging from the sea between Sicily and Tunisia, the 32-square-mile island of Pantelleria is an impregnable barley twist of volcanic rhyolite. Seams of copper and orange bookend its black cliffs like moving lightning. And everything is covered in 1,000-year-old Arabic terraces of vines and capers, so teeming with trans-Saharan winds that the branches crawl close to the ground in a gnarled bonsai swoon. Little hamlets of lava-stone-domed houses called dammusi have been built down the centuries to resemble scarab beetles, with windows like gashes and gardens of cactuses stalked by sulking cockerels.

A succession of cultures have possessed Pantelleria. Vandals, Carthaginians, pirates. Once everybody spoke Arabic but prayed as Christians, trading with North Africa, and Jewish merchants, and Basilian monks. Now the island is Sicilian-Catholic, and yet is coolly lazy about religion. Suspended between Africa and Europe, it looks to neither mainland with particular longing.

In the main harbour there's a stall that sells just-dried chillies and savage hunks of pork under a decades-old picture of Jesus dissolving blondely into his halo. I'm biding my time, waiting for Pasticceria Gelateria Katia along the waterfront to start serving its dark-chocolate gelato, nubby with Pantescan capers so dense and fragrant you comprehend that they are in fact edible flower buds, real knots of life. In the glass cases of the shop, when it opens, are cannoli stuffed with a great quantity of a moon-pale ricotta, like bulging Edwardian corsets, which the owner piles carefully, one by one, into a white box for an impatient woman dressed up for a wedding. The door bangs open and shut, the sound of church bells and outboard motors churning the harbour beyond.

The port at Scauri is prettier. A bar-café, called Kaya Kaya, sits on sanded boards just above the rocks selling cubes of swordfish shining with marinated orange and oil, and caponata full of pine nuts the size of clout nails. The morning falls on the water below with merciless clarity. From the tiny café kitchen a radio pounds out old tunes, Bryan Ferry singing "Kiss and Tell" with his buttery mouth as the blue of the sky spreads like a fan. Down on the rocks a few children take running leaps and vault themselves into the warm sea, lying on their backs and floating in a dreamlike lostness, occasionally reaching out a hand to check they're not too close to the rocks – they can be sharp. But it's swimming off rocks or nothing; there are no beaches here. A friend in Palermo who came to the island every summer through the 1960s tells stories about diving for sea urchins from these rocks when he was 15. He would bring them up and slice them open like passion fruit, dipping them in the salted olive oil he had decanted into holes in the honeycombed stone, his feet and hands leathery from the jags and brine. "It's a kind of paradise on Pantelleria," he told me, "but nothing is... easy." He'd stabbed his fist quickly into the air, as though demonstrating the most overwhelming of feelings. "Everything there is like a knife. *Affilato*."

One day I meet with a woman called Arianne, a fifty-something Sicilian friend of a friend who's lived mostly on the island for decades. Her battered hatchback is scattered with old letters and cigarette lighters and gummed-together boiled sweets, and when I ask her to show me her favourite hidden Pantescan thing she screws up her eyes against the light and heads down narrow roads exploding with Judas trees. The khaki hillsides are latticed with crumbling stone walls, wild fennel reaching so thick and featherishly into the wound-down windows we eventually get out and walk through the area of Mueggen, heat dazzling off fields of volcanic soil planted with little round aubergines and sweet Zibibbo grapes that make a fantastically mellow passito. "Here, taste," orders Arianne, passing me some as we stoop by a vine, the grapes dropping into my hand like hot stones. (Someone told me that Arianne is a princess. Sicilians are obsessed with nobility. My old boyfriend, Luca, is always grumbling about it. "This baron and that prince, with their crests and villa with no roof. My great grandmother had the same name as a duke! *Ma chi se ne frega!*") By the time we come to a grove of oak trees the mid-afternoon sky is a roofless blue vault. Beneath us, carved deep into rocks, is a trio of Byzantine tombs, each touchingly modest, as though three delicate people had just come to lie down for a while among the crunching dried acorns and dandelions. In the field beyond, a song thrush buffets against the wind, like a speck of thrown seed.

One of my favourite films, *A Bigger Splash*, was made on the island in 2015 – about a British rock singer hiding out from the world, and wrangling her troublesome lovers. In one scene a housekeeper puffs out her cheeks as she battles from a car, hooting, "I don't even know what wind it is today!" All kinds of winds collide on Pantelleria. The mistral with the sirocco, and that's just two of the ones I've heard of. (The island is known in Arabic as "Daughter of the Wind".) Islanders stand in the street looking at an app on their phones that details the latest knots and turbulence, their eyes narrowed to fascinated slits, garments wrenched up and fluttering behind their prone bodies, like wings. I stay for a few days at the place where they made that film – an elegant estate called Tenuta Borgia, with dammusi renovated to feel almost like tranquil chapels and polished gargantuan beds spread with laundered white lace. The grounds are full of vines and vibrant majolica ceramics and crimson hibiscus. A walled Arabic garden has a citrus tree that catches the movement of the light through the day as though it were a sundial.

You get to like the wind. One evening I battle up the Via Sotto Kuddia in Scauri, scarcely able to walk in a straight line against gusts so warm and powerful it feels like I'm moving through thick velvet curtains. After a while I give up and sit on a pavement watching two elderly women at a table by an open door as they wait for someone to bring dinner up the steep steps from the Panettiere Marrone Francesco below – the best pizza on the island, studded with sweet onion. I'd been at a christening party all day, where 40 islanders in enormous sunglasses had stood swaying to Van Morrison and The Marvelettes while they brought out great platters of sugared almonds, and oregano sausages, and rabbit stewed in passito. After a lot of wine and many espressos, everybody passed around the well-padded baby, his mother wearing an ingeniously arty dress made from what might have been swagged fishing nets, with iridescent shells on a string, strands of hair curling damply at the nape of her neck, like a mermaid who'd only emerged that morning. Everybody had danced and talked a lot, and been less brusque and sceptical than usual – Pantescans are not sentimental. They are fatalistic; their eyebrows are perpetually raised. Coloured lanterns along the bar were dim and lustrous, and when I left I passed an old man with a long beard descending the darkening hill carrying a loaf of bread in the moonlight, like a saint.

The best cinema in Italy is on Pantelleria. In the Cineteatro San Gaetano's tiny deco lobby, Marlon Brando smirks in a framed still from *The Wild One*, hung on the wall over a rusting Veronese projector. The place literally vibrates with the drumfire and rumble of the evening feature. Giorgio Armani paid for the new sound system, and it's IMAX intense, the whole place a pullulating boom box run by teenage boys – ushers with otter-slicked pseudo-hipster hair – who just about tolerate the attentions of diva-ish younger sisters of friends dropping by to flirt until the movie ends and they all scooter home, jabbering about escaping to college in Naples. Armani has been coming to the island for years. If you've ever wondered about the obsessive rigour of the designer's palette, it's all Pantelleria. His thousand shades of black and silver, the boldness, the theatre, it's here in the rock. His villa overlooks Gadir, a hamlet at the bottom of a cliff where natural hot springs edge a cove by the sea.

Pantelleria is staggeringly elemental. Inside it boils with fumaroles and volcanic springs. When I stayed at the island's most beautiful hotel, Sikelia, a waiter said to me, "Come and see Africa," and led me up some steps to the gently domed roof, and then turned with a tremendous flourish to the horizon, which seemed at first to be a dense string of ravingly jumping candle flames. The sun was setting 27 miles to the west over Tunisia. For over an hour the immense spreading redness went on, brutal. Triumphant as an unrepentant martyr roasting on hot coals. Eventually it puffed itself out, leaving the same stunned aura of burnt wicks and smoke at the end of a firework display. *Everything is like a knife. Affilato.*

When Luca comes to meet me for a few days, we drive the island back and forth in an old Mini Moke-like Citroën Méhari (they're everywhere here) with grinding back-to-front gears, playing Captain Beefheart on a loop in tribute to Matthias Schoenaerts in *A Bigger Splash*, who negotiated so sexily the pitted tracks and potholes of the island's hills, flooring the clutch in trodden-down deck shoes while Tilda Swinton hung off his neck. How do Pantescans differ from other Sicilians, I ask Luca, and he sets his mouth like Empedocles, and nods. "In Sicily we always worry we're about to be screwed. But here it's more a case of we're screwed anyway – so relax." The flowing fields of capers around us give way to swathes of amber flowers that look like waving hedgerows of Champagne.

High above the village of Siba, in caves with natural saunas, we find a whole family sitting inside, steaming away, eating nectarines. And a young soldier who'd come all the way from Rome on a motorbike. The dialect in some of these remoter villages is full of the remnants of pre-Islamic words, which sound like little psalms. *Cinciuki* – I am soaked by the rain. *Milakhi* – I feel tired, and thoughtful.

Later, we drive on to the lagoon in the middle of the mountains – the Mirror of Venus – an ancient caldera coloured the outlandish blue of a Himalayan poppy and edged by a few bathers crusted in skin-softening mud, standing still and pensive as herons. The smell of sulphur hangs lightly in the air when we get there and the enfolding circle of hills is covered in crumbling stone terraces. Dipped out of the wind and stretching away 500 metres in front of us, the warm lake is like a magic carpet so vibrant and unlikely it looks as though some toddlers got together and drew it. We eat hunks of pasta and pancetta still warm from the dawn oven from the Terremoto bakery in Khamma, and go to order Indian-fig granita at the one café on the lake shore. Giant *cucuzza* are drying along its windowsills, and in the garden bursting spikes of agave grow high as a door.

Sinatra sings "Mack the Knife" somewhere in a parked van and two little boys in Superman Y-fronts play Frisbee with their brown dog, yelling his name with love – Greco! Greco! – all down the dusty track. Heat and dust and friendly lizards. Without the wind, says Luca, you don't half notice the sun. My friend Irene says she once burned so badly on the island she felt her back might slide off, but her room-mate quickly administered a local remedy, covering her all over in slices of raw potato to draw out the heat. When they came off her – near-cooked – the following morning, the skin beneath was soft and healed. This is supremely Pantescan. Hot but verdant. Dry but lush. One time, out in a small boat, the sea was clear to

20 ravishing metres and the land that loomed beyond looked iron-bound. By an outcrop called Sirens Cove, the sea moaned against the rocks, like music. The captain produced a hunk of local stone he'd polished, called Pantellerite, black as quartz, and yet at its core another colour flares. "See!" he said, holding it up to the sun and twisting it about, as though it were a just-found gem. "See how its heart is green."

AN ACT
OF FAITH

Stephanie Cavagnaro

For *National Geographic Traveller*
July 2018

Amleamo is committed. She decided to wake up this morning and wear red – all red. Her outfit spans shades of crimson and claret: from T-shirt and fleece to ankle-length skirt and big woolly hat askew on her head, revealing unruly salt-and-pepper hair. Even her teeth are red, stained by a lifetime of chewing *doma* (areca nut and betel leaf), which she spits sporadically on to the pavement, its juice collecting next to her in small puddles.

Her commitment to her ensemble is a sartorial expression of her larger commitment to her faith: she's visited Jambay Lhakhang – one of Bhutan's oldest temples – every single day for the past 18 years, she says, instinctively spinning a handheld prayer wheel. A garland of wooden beads with tassels is spread across her lap, used to keep track of mantras. When I ask the current count, she fumbles with the beads and scrunches up her face, making the deep lines carved by her 78 years more prominent. It takes her a moment before she answers: two million in two years.

"The most important thing in Buddhism is rebirth," explains Tshering, my portly guide who wears a knee-length *gho*, the national dress for men. "The best way is to pray for your future because you don't know tomorrow," he adds, as Amleamo begins thumbing her beads and mumbling mantras to the Guru Rinpoche.

You don't have to travel far in Bhutan to see images of this mustachioed Buddhist master. Regarded as the second Buddha, the Guru Rinpoche founded Tibetan Buddhism in the eighth century and is revered for spreading the religion across this Vajrayana stronghold – a school of Buddhism particular to Tibet and select neighbouring Himalayan regions.

Religious conventions still wield a strong influence over life in this mountainous kingdom. It's peppered with thousands of monuments and monasteries, while handmade *chorten* (stupas) crowd remote caves, bald-headed monks pray in temples, and clusters of white prayer flags mounted on poles dance on windy mountains. "We believe animals can hear the sound of the prayer flags, and in the next life they are reborn as human beings and have a better life," says Tshering.

Perhaps in order to preserve its unique identity, the country sat in isolation for years, only opening to visitors in 1974. It currently charges a steep daily fee of $250 (£179) for all-inclusive organised tours – a cost-induced exclusivity that means Bhutan is often blissfully crowd-free. The tourist tax is just one way the country has kept environmental conservation high on its political agenda. Government decrees say that 60 per cent of the kingdom's land must be forested; plastic bags are prohibited; and mountaineering was banned in 2003.

This enthusiasm for eco is especially evident here in Bumthang, a mountainous, Switzerland-in-Asia central region that's packed with alpine forests and broad, fertile valleys covered in fields of buckwheat. This bucolic area is the religious heartland of the nation with some of its oldest temples – many of which are linked to Guru Rinpoche's visit over 1,000 years ago.

"Bumthang is considered one of the holiest places in Bhutan," adds Tshering. And this temple is one of its holiest highlights. Jambay Lhakhang is made up of a series of square orange and white buildings topped by golden roofs. It doesn't hide its age: stones have come loose from its facade, while cracks creep into intricate carvings that frame the doors and windows. Prayer wheels are inscribed with ancient scripture, handles worn by the devout who have kept them spinning for centuries. Around the squat buildings are little silver stupas containing handwritten prayers and plastic cups with stones used for counting circumambulations.

Built in AD 659, Jambay Lhakhang is one of numerous temples simultaneously constructed on top of a demon, according to legend. "The demon's body covered all the Himalayas," explains Tshering. "One hundred and eight temples were built to hold the demon down – we are here on the left knee."

This ancient place seems to attract fittingly ancient devotees. "Whatever they committed – a mistake or sin – during their young age, they're trying to clean it up," Tshering explains. I watch an elderly man wearing pink polka-dot pyjamas and a glitter-blue hat walk clockwise around the temple. When he heads inside to pray, I slip off my shoes, and follow him towards a sunny courtyard.

Inside, I spot an old woman with a laminated image of Guru Rinpoche among her possessions. She's mumbling mantras while moving in half-prostrations on a mat; her hands are in the shape of a lotus bud, which she places on her head, to her throat and her heart before dropping to her knees and lowering her head to the ground. "If we shower, we clean only the outer part. It's different to clean inner part," instructs Tshering, adding that prostrations are a means of purifying the body, speech and mind of karmic sins.

Flanking the old woman are dark circles on the pavement – imprints of knees and a forehead left by former pilgrims. "That's like, one hundred thousand times – the marks there," says Tshering as the woman finishes praying. She picks up her mat and shuffles out of the temple, spinning a large prayer wheel as she goes. Its loud dinging fills the reverential silence.

EYE OF THE TIGER

"The Bhutanese people, they try to visit once in their life," Tshering declares as we walk through dense pine forest festooned with prayer flags on my last day in Bhutan. The scenery is alluring, but I can't stop myself from looking up at our destination – the Tiger's Nest, a Buddhist monastery clinging to a near-vertical cliff 10,232 ft above the lush western Paro valley.

It's claimed that the Guru Rinpoche arrived to this sacred site from Tibet on the back of a flying tigress. "He came to Paro to subdue the local deity," adds Tshering, who has swapped his dress shoes for hiking boots. This complex was then built in 1692 around the cave where the great sage meditated.

Though we're steadily climbing through cloud forest, the monastery looms above – and without a flying tiger, it's a leg-taxing ascent of over 1,700 ft. There isn't vehicle access and horsepower only delivers pilgrims halfway, so we trudge skyward with locals and claret-robed monks through pines draped with tendrils of moss. In this thin mountain air, my shallow gulps are mocked by a giggling white-throated laughing thrush.

But over an hour's hike has brought me to a clearing in the bottle-green forest – and at eye level with the Tiger's Nest whose golden pinnacles and red rooftops are set over whitewashed walls that cling to granite ledges. The buildings are on the opposite ravine, so I hike down stone steps and over a 200-ft waterfall that nosedives towards the valley. Icicles break free from the rock face, and as the sun hits them, they sparkle like glitter. From the vantage of a wooden bridge, the valley unfolds – golden light casts an ethereal glow on tree-covered mountains and sacred, snowy peaks. Prayer flags with tattered ends that have been eaten by a hungry wind are strung precipitously over a deep gorge.

Steep steps finally deposit my altitude-racked remains at the sanctuary with its series of nine temples and chambers carved into the rock. I take off my shoes before heading towards incense that wafts through thin air from within a room. "We call this the wish-fulfilling temple," Tshering tells me. The focal point is a giant golden statue of Rinpoche, whose head is cocked to one side indicating that he's listening. An altar is crammed with Buddhist iconography and heaped with offerings: water, incense, milk, crisps, money, burning butter lamps. Artistic ritual cakes are made up of circular patterns intricately painted all the colours of the spectrum.

Locals in their national dress stream in; I take my place against the wall and listen to the soft thudding of knees and heads on the floor. One mother places a note in her baby's hand as an offering; another worshipper adds a block of butter to the table, which a monk gratefully accepts before pouring holy water into her hands; she brings it to her lips, slurps and splashes the remainder on the crown of her head. Another woman begins full prostrations, taking up the width of the floor once horizontal.

I tiptoe between temples, my feet growing numb on frigid stone. One contains gold pillars surrounding a hole piled high with money. "Some say the Guru Rinpoche died in there, some say he subdued the local deity there," explains Tshering. A monk approaches, pulls a twenty-Bhutanese-ngultrum note out of his wallet, touches it to his head and drops it. "This should be the bank of Taktsang [Tiger's Nest]," jokes Tshering.

"Now we go to the last one," he adds, ushering me towards the Temple of Longevity. I head to a window on the far side and my heart races as I look a few thousand feet directly down at the pine-packed valley floor. I turn back to the altar, which has three statues of Buddha, as a family enters carrying a bag of rice. A young boy takes a handful, bows his head to the altar and sprinkles his offering on a bowl of notes. I ask Tshering what the pious are expected to offer in temples. "Whatever you do, your heart should be pure," he replies.

We leave this temple, and head towards an opening in the cliff. A small sign above it reads "Tiger's Nest". Tshering tells me this is the place where the tiger supposedly rested during the guru's meditation, and warns me about the tricky descent into the deep cave crevice. I'm not much of a speleologist, but I'm curious, so I leave Tshering behind and slide across a slanted wooden panel before crawling down a ladder wedged between rocks. I squeeze around the ladder and drop into a giant slice of cliff.

There's a crack in the precipice to one side with a vertical drop, so I head blindly the other way, feebly feeling damp rocks to guide me through the dark. I squint towards the outline of a huddled family. When they stand up to leave, a monk and I flatten ourselves against a wall to let them pass. I blink against jet-black darkness as the light of a solitary butter lamp comes into focus, illuminating a small shrine with white ceremonial silk scarves and a picture of Rinpoche. As the lamp flickers, I think of all the lights brightly burning across this Himalayan kingdom and Tshering's simple words about their significance: "Whoever is in darkness, it clears the way."

BULLS
AND
SCARS

—

Nick Hunt

For *Dark Mountain*
October 2018

In this place, Kucha says, the women are whipped by the men.
   Whipped? I ask.
   Yes, with sticks. Until their backs are bleeding.

———————————

I am not at all sure that I want to go to the Omo Valley. Or – if I'm being honest – I want to go there very much. The desire is like an ache, twisting when I think of it, inducing a kind of breathlessness that makes me slightly dizzy. It is a feeling very much like falling bravely in love, when you know that to turn away will make you somehow smaller. For the past four months I have worked in a small Ethiopian town and now I have travelled south where everything is different. The highlands and the misty air, the churches cut from solid rock, the mountains and the monasteries, disappeared days ago. The land ahead is yellow, sparse, and intensely tribal. The people who live in this terrain – to my eyes, a glaring desert that can hardly support life – are bewilderingly diverse. Each has found a radically different way to be human. There are women who stretch their lips with enormous clay plates. Men who gorge on blood and milk to make themselves competitively fat. People who alter their physical forms by scarification and modification to express their cultural uniqueness, to tell the world *We are who we are, and not anybody else.* I am curious to see such people because they sound extraordinary. But I am not sure whether I really should.

The reason for my doubt is not to do with women being whipped, because I do not know about this yet. It is to do with what I have heard referred to as *tribal safaris*: rich white people paying hundreds of dollars to be ferried in convoys of 4x4s to throw money at tribal people while they dance and wear ceremonial costumes. Everything about it sounds exploitative, gross and wrong. I have told myself I will come this far – to the edge of the Omo Valley, a city called Arba Minch, which means Forty Springs – to see how things look from here. Maybe it is different up close. Maybe there is another way.

There is. His name is Kucha and he introduces himself in a bar. He has a deep scar down one side of his face and the air of a desperado. He says his mother was from one of the tribes and he understands the people here, knows how to move around the land. We won't travel by private vehicle but hitch lifts on trucks supplying the villages deep in the desert. We will sleep in truckers' motels, travel cheaply and take our chances. We will avoid other tourists. He grins and swigs from a bottle of beer. He is clearly not trustworthy. But he is convincing. Early next morning we are on a truck thundering through monotonous scrub, trailing a plume of white dust like the wake behind a ship.

The truck bounces on and on. Kucha doesn't speak very much. The whites of his eyes are red from staying up drinking half the night with the first part of the money I paid him. He keeps one side of his face turned away, and later I see that his lip is split and his left cheek is badly bruised. Some trouble, he shrugs when I ask. Later his mood improves.

The truck halts at a tiny village and we get out and wait for a long time, drinking sweet fizzy drinks, and then get into another truck that continues down the same road. We switch rides throughout the day, weaving our way further and further into the vast land. The places at which we stop are outposts of an incoming culture: truck stops full of hard, sullen men; plastic tables and plastic chairs; flies; casual AK-47s; things being loaded and unloaded; things being bought and sold. The air is hot and thick with dust, heavy with waiting. Roads look big when you are on them and small when you are far away. Beyond this poorly tarmacked strip, which appears so slim in the immensity it wanders through, it is easy to believe that this encroachment has had no impact. There are village roofs thatched with grass; women walking in the bush with long, loping strides; herds of pale cattle flicking their enormous horns; very tall, very dark-skinned men watching the noisy vehicles pass with no expressions on their faces. Kucha tells me what tribe they are from, how they live in relation to others. We chew *khat* to pass the time, which produces a sense of mild euphoria cut with buzzing urgency, a desire to smoke lots of cigarettes and munch salted peanuts.

The beast below us jolts and sways. This is the last truck of the day and it will carry us through the night. We are sitting high on top of the load, on tightly packed sacks of rice, with six or seven other men dangling their legs over the sides. Occasionally one of them sings quietly over the engine noise. With a sack of rice for a pillow and sacks of rice for a bed I am shaken to sleep as the sun goes down. Later I wake to impossible stars and the motherly rumble of the truck and the knowledge that no one in the world knows where in the world I am. The continent spreads like a vast dark sea. I feel numb with joy. This is one of the purest moments of happiness I will know.

———————

Always this sense when travelling: *Will I find it here? Will the great secret reveal itself? Is it around the next corner?* There is never anything around the next corner except the next corner but sometimes I catch fragments of it, this fleeting thing I am looking for. *That mountainside, that's a part of it there. The way the light falls on that wall. That old man sitting under a mulberry tree with his dog sleeping at his feet, that's a part of the secret too.* If I could fit these pieces together I would be completed.

Waking on these sacks of rice I nearly see the shape of it. The outlines of the secret loom, extraordinary and almost whole. I can almost touch it. I think: *Yes, this is it, I am here, I have arrived*. But I have not arrived. I am travelling too fast. The moment has already gone. The truck rolls onwards through the night and the secret slides away.

Kucha takes me to places that confound my preconceptions. He shows me things I will never forget, and things I would rather not see.

We are in a battered bus going up a long hill to see some kind of celebration of the breaking of a fast. Kucha says casually: They will slaughter bulls for the feast.

How many bulls? I ask, imagining maybe two or three.

Two hundred, he says, and I think he is joking or has got his numbers wrong until we reach the top of the hill and see the field of blood. A large crowd is gathered here. There is great jollity. The bulls are led, sweet-eyed and calm, into the centre of the field to have their throats cut with machetes. The process is both quicker and slower than I would have thought possible. They slump forwards, bellowing. I see their profound confusion. Some of them attempt to charge but lose strength very quickly. Within minutes their carcasses are processed by knifemen of great skill: they are beheaded, skinned, dehorned, dehooved, gutted and defleshed, divided into neat components; slabs of pale pinkish meat, marbled fat and purple organs are laid on banana leaves to be admired and bartered for. The grass is swampy with blood. It looks like the aftermath of a medieval battle. Men and women eat raw meat and drink honey wine. People stagger, drunk on meat. The scale of the slaughter is so immense that my mind shuts it out. *We are humans, they are bulls,* that's all I can really think. I am offered a cube of flesh. It tastes bland, like sushi.

Kucha takes me to a village of tall drystone walls that wind like a labyrinth to confuse invaders. The walls are beautifully constructed from large grey stones, an architecture unlike anything else for 1,000 miles. No one knows where, in this continent, these people came here from, bringing a language and traditions that bear no relation to anyone else's. Outside a communal building sits a group of men wearing brightly patterned clothes and sipping out of hollow gourds. They invite us to sit with them. They are aloof but amiable; I feel more relaxed in their company than I have felt for weeks. One of the gourds is passed to me. It is full of sour porridge made from a fermented grain. Suddenly I understand the distant, tranquil atmosphere: the porridge is mildly alcoholic and everyone is slightly drunk. This is their staple food, which they consume throughout the day. I decide that I like it here, in this village of serene, permanently half-cut porridge sippers. But Kucha is keen to get away. I tell him we should stay a while, maybe ask to spend the night. He insists that we leave. We argue. He wins, of course. I follow him grudgingly.

On the way back down the hill he tells me that these people killed his father in a disagreement about the ownership of cattle.

I know nothing about anything. It's a relief to admit this now and let myself be led. All I see is the surface of things – the elaborate hairstyle of a man, shaved to the crown and plastered down in a clay-hardened bun; a woman's goatskin skirt fringed with cowrie shells – and not the complex layers of meaning that lie beneath. I understand nothing of the ways in which these things fit together, how they collide or overlap. There are symbols I cannot read, lines I do not see.

We have reached a marketplace where men and women display their wares on rugs laid on the beaten ground. The area is rather small but people have walked for days to be here in order to hear important news about births, deaths, cattle, the weather, tribal politics. Older men are sitting on carved wooden stools in the shade of acacia trees, discussing matters earnestly. This is not a marginal place but the centre of a world. The women have tightly braided hair thickly smeared with orange clay. Their bare backs have a texture that I don't understand at first, and only when we get closer do I see that it is scar tissue.

I have a camera in my hand. I want to remember everything. *Will the great secret reveal itself? Is a fragment of it here?* One day, an anthropologist studying late-stage Western consumerist culture might be able to explain my compulsion to take that picture. I am pointing my camera at a woman I do not know, whose life I do not understand, in conversation with her friends. As I press the button she turns and looks at me directly. She says something sharp and hard. I feel as if I have been hit by a rock. She stares at me as I back away, mumbling apologies. I feel like a thief who has been caught committing a pathetic crime. I am embarrassed for myself and my stupid culture.

An approaching cloud of dust. A fleet of white 4x4s. Their air-conditioned interiors disgorge the crudest stereotypes of tourists I have ever seen: a sweat-spotted blimp of a man, white socks pulled up to his knees, sticking a camera in an old man's face and bellowing, *Hello, photo!*; a six-foot blonde in tiny clothes holding her mobile phone with one hand and her nose with the other; a man aiming a telephoto lens at a woman breastfeeding her baby. It is as if my own disrespectful and invasive act has somehow summoned them, avatars of the grossest aspects of my civilisation.

A friend of mine refuses to travel to countries poorer than his own. Not because he is scared of robbery or disease, but because the inequality implicit in every human exchange induces a squirming awkwardness and corrosive sense of guilt. For him, the power disparity overshadows everything: every conversation, every handshake, every smile and gesture. He would rather not travel than be in that situation.

I have always argued against this view, because to see all human interactions as a function of economics means accepting capitalism in its totality, denying that people are driven by forces other than power and greed, excluding the possibility of there being anything else. The grotesque display of these photographic trophy hunters makes me think of him now. Their presence – my presence – here would seem to prove his point: economically powerful Westerners are using the force field of their wealth to behave in a way that they wouldn't back home, to humiliate and commodify economically poor tribal people. And yet, there is something else going on. The line is not that simple.

As the marketplace disappears in the rear-view mirror of another truck, I am struck by conflicting images. These are the ones that stay with me: foreigners staggering in the heat, waterfalls of sweat pouring off them, absurdly out of place; tribespeople giggling, pointing, either mocking their ridiculous guests or else completely ignoring them; intense vulnerability on one hand and intense confidence on the other. The elaborate costumes on display are not worn for photographs. Every scar, every hairstyle, every bodily adornment says *This is who we are* and *We are not you*. The disparity is not so much of wealth but of belonging. Those who belong, who have always belonged, and those who are profoundly displaced. It destroys my preconceptions. I find myself feeling sorry not for the poor exploited tribe but for the desperate, unsatisfied tourists. And a little for myself.

The young man is naked, tall, grave and covered in grey dust. The bulls are lined up side by side, swishing horns at one end and swishing tails at the other. The man must leap from back to back, keeping his balance as they shift, up and down the muscled line until the women are satisfied. This is to prove that he is brave and eligible for marriage.

This takes place in a clearing in a patch of acacia trees, near a dried-out riverbed a half-hour walk from the road. There are hundreds of people here, an air of great celebration, a continual blowing of horns and jangling of bells. The tourists are here as well – the same group as yesterday – but their significance has shrunk and I hardly notice them. The jumper of bulls is the centre around which everything revolves, and outsiders are exactly that: outsiders, permitted to observe, because this ritual is a point of pride and obvious importance.

Kucha and I are standing next to a neatly dressed engineer working for a Chinese company building telecommunications infrastructure, the only other guest at our flyblown, breeze block-walled hotel. He is Ethiopian but an urbanite from the north, which makes him as foreign as I am. He is astonished by everything. Kucha is in his element in the role of raconteur.

It is now that we hear about the whipping of the women.

The men jump over bulls, Kucha says, and the women are whipped. It is their way of doing things here.

Until their backs are bleeding.

This explains the scar tissue on the women's backs and across their bellies, accumulated over the years. Young women have only a few scars; older women are tracked with them. The engineer is as horrified as me. From both our points of view there is no possible way to see this as anything other than the rankest misogyny, a ritualised brutality aimed at demonstrating men's power, men's right to inflict pain, and women's subjugation. My mind will not be changed on this. There can be no other perspective.

Once again, I understand nothing. All my preconceptions are about to be destroyed again.

————————

A woman who is harder than any other woman I have seen before – a woman who could fling a word like a rock and knock me out with it – thrusts a switch of wood at a hesitant young man. He grins reluctantly, holding it. She bares her back to him, covered in years of scars. He does nothing. She yells at him. He gives her a few half-hearted whacks and tries to put the switch away. Seizing it from his hands, she hurls it away and gives him a larger one. He looks around uncertainly. Other women jeer at him. He hits her again, a little harder. She cajoles him furiously and it is obvious, in any language, what she is saying: *Do it harder. You are a coward. Don't be so weak. Do it more.* Once he is in the rhythm of it and her back is wet with blood, the other women shout compliments. Finally she has had enough. Her face shows fury but not pain. Scornfully she turns away, without another glance at him, and goes to rejoin her friends. He leaves with obvious relief. Blood is spotted on the earth. Another woman picks up a switch and scans the crowd.

I do not understand this at the time, because I am still seeing what I have expected to see: men more powerful than women treating women terribly. It takes a little time for my eyes to override my brain. Only later, thinking about this day, do different connections form. This is not men saying to women: *We are stronger than you*. It is women saying to men: *We are as strong as you. We can take the pain*. If men are to be celebrated for jumping on the backs of bulls, women insist on proving their ability to endure. This is necessary, perhaps. Life here is extremely hard. There are tribal wars, and cattle raids, and wild animals, and drought. People who cannot accept that pain is a part of life – people who do not step into it, to learn what their bodies are capable of – are about as much use as the waddling tourists.

Of course, life is changing here. There are things I do not see. The Chinese roads and the power lines; the dams across the Omo River; the telecommunications infrastructure that the engineer has come to build; the true cargo of the trucks, which is not rice or sorghum flour but the shrinking of time and space and exposure to capitalism, alcohol, prostitution and AIDS; the effects of climate change; the desert expanding year by year; the vanishing wildlife; the impact of outside influence, not today, as I have witnessed it, but ten or twenty years down the line when the old men under the acacia trees are gone and the young men jumping bulls have grown up to take their place – when the women with few scars have become women with many scars – in an environment that can only grow more hostile.

But preconceptions can be destroyed. I have learned that twice. Who is really vulnerable here? Who has the power that matters? The people who expose themselves to pain, and contain it in ritualised forms, or the people who seek to insulate themselves from all discomfort? Those who belong, and have always belonged, or those who are displaced? On the hard ground that lies ahead, which culture will endure?

They say that travelling opens doors, gives people new perspectives. This is only partially true. People carry their doors with them; perspectives seldom truly change. But my friend is wrong. If we stay within our horizons, surrounded by people who are the same as us, it precludes all hope. We shut off any possibility of having our automatic beliefs – whether good or bad, right or wrong – smashed so their rubble can make new shapes. We will never be forced to understand that there are different ways to be human, different ways to be ourselves. And we desperately need that knowledge, even if we don't know it yet.

Always this sense when travelling: *Will I find it here?* We are back on the road again, leaving the Omo Valley. Kucha's weary, bloodshot eyes are fixed on the horizon line. The enormity of land flows past, liquidised by the speed of travel. The great secret lies around the next corner, as it always will.

A DICTIONARY FOR PAST PLANTS

———

Jessica J. Lee

For *Caught by the River*
November 2019

The bajiao stood at the end of an orchard field neighbouring the cemetery. Its leaves were broad and glossy, pale green in the hot light. No other trees like it grew nearby; in the orchard, only dragonfruit cactuses grew, their fruits pink and wrapped in plastic. I thought the bajiao looked lonely.

"What is it?" I asked my mother.《芭 蕉》she replied.

Bajiao. I stretched its shape into my mouth, and then asked again what the tree was.

"False banana," my mother concluded in English. She then turned her attention to the cemetery, where my grandfather's ashes had been interred four years earlier.

The 芭 蕉 was the first plant she taught me in Taiwan. *Musa basjoo*, a small tree bearing inedible bananas. Surely I had seen it in Europe or North America – in garden centres and ornamental displays – but in its field in southern Taiwan, it seemed foreign to me. I felt foreign, too, though my mother had been born and raised there.

My mother had taught me at a young age to pay attention to plants. There were plants I knew well, temperate plants that grew in the places I visited often: heather and gorse, Scots pine and plane trees. Theirs was a language I spoke. When we reached Taiwan – a place I had long imagined but never known well – I felt more inarticulate than ever.

My grandfather was the first plant lover among us. At least, that's what I know for sure; perhaps he learned from his parents or grandparents back in China. He kept a small garden during my childhood and tended to the curling bonsai tree that grew in the dining room. My mother once told me that when he'd first moved to Taiwan at the end of the Chinese civil war, leaving his family and past behind him, he'd planted banana trees in his garden. He'd needed urgently for something to take root.

We took a taxi into Kaohsiung, where my mother was born and my grandfather had died, and from the window my mother pointed to another new name: 鳳凰木 (*fenghuang mu*). She translated it literally: the phoenix tree.

The phoenix tree stood near ten metres tall, casting an umbrella of shade onto the busy sidewalk. Sprays of feathery green leaves hung from its crown, with scarlet flowers laced among the branches. I took a photograph and wrote out its name as my mother had pronounced it.

Hours later, I looked up "phoenix tree" but could find nothing of the red-flowered city tree I had seen. I asked my mother to help me type its name in Chinese characters, and only then could I find it, backtracking from the Chinese Wikipedia entry to the tree's English entry: *Delonix regia*, often called "royal Poinciana". Once I'd learned its name, I began to see the phoenix tree everywhere.

I wondered then how my mother could remember all these names: she had emigrated from Taiwan 40 years earlier, settling in southern Ontario, where I was born. The plants she saw often in her life in Canada had little in common with the brimming tropical hues that burst from the verges in Taiwan. But I realised how much she must have missed this overflow of life. How the winter – with six months of snow and bare branch – must have pained her.

Seeking green, my mother and I ventured to the southern tip of the country, where a waterfall with seven pools spun from the foothills into a coral plateau. At their base, we found another lone tree. It grew at the end of a rutted lane watched over by kind stray dogs. The tree's trunk was dusted with grey and gold lichen, but its rounded leaves shone bottle green. Amongst them hung fine filaments of white and pink, paintbrush-like flowers bursting forth in huge clusters. Where the blooms had fallen back, pale green box fruits hung heavy.

This was a tree we both had to look up: 玉蕊 (pronounced "yurui"). The "jade stamen tree" or *Barringtonia asiatica*. Together, we memorised its name, then studied its past: like my family, the tree was considered curiously as both introduced and native to Taiwan.

The yurui had travelled here by sea: a migrant tree, its sturdy green fruit floats until it reaches new shores. Coconuts, for example, do much the same. Travelling the southern sea, they can remain afloat for up to fifteen years.

But eventually washed ashore in a new place – some distant home – the yurui tree takes root.

RIDING THE
REUNIFICATION
EXPRESS

Emma Thomson

For *National Geographic Traveller*
March 2019

"We're no longer a country of war – we've moved on," declares our guide, Mr Tien. I believe him. All around us, swarms of commuters are hunched over their scooter handlebars as if leaning toward the future. Following the throng into the heart of the capital Hanoi, we pass elderly couples waltzing in the park, a lady and her poodle with matching tie-dye hairdos and high-school girls sporting slogan T-shirts and a flash of red lipstick.

The bus halts and I step into a fog of frying chillies and fuel. Before me, a brash block of concrete obscures the historic canary-yellow side wings of Vietnam's oldest railway station. Passengers tug their suitcases behind them like unruly dogs, seemingly oblivious to the conflicts this pile of bricks and mortar has witnessed since it was erected in 1902. A B-52 carpet bombing during the Vietnam War hit it hardest, obliterating the central hall. It was rebuilt as it's seen today in 1976 – the very same year the once communist north and democratic south were reunified following the north's victory and 20 years of civil war. A historic moment consolidated, rather uniquely, by a pair of parallel metal lines.

Some structures come to define a nation. For Vietnam, that is the North–South railway line known as the Reunification Express – a 1,072-mile-long steel spinal cord that curves the length of the country from Hanoi in the far north to the southern metropolis of Ho Chi Minh (still called Saigon by locals). Its formation and history mirror the fluctuating fortunes of the country and to ride these rails is to traverse not only timelines of major events, but also religious and cultural divides between the Catholic north with its French vibe and the Buddhist south with American influences.

The first tracks were laid in 1899 under French colonial rule with the (unsuccessful) aim of stealing the lucrative Indochina rice market away from shipping companies. It took another 30 years to piece together the separately constructed sections, but jobs-for-life with steady salaries were flowing and the proverb on everyone's lips was: "If you want a good life, marry a railway man."

In 1936 a locomotive travelled the entire length of the Transindochinois line – as it was known – for the first time. The journey took 60 hours, but passengers had a cinema car and even a hairdressing salon aboard to help pass the time.

Later "the railway tracks became the rope in the tug of war for power during the Vietnam War," says Tim Doling, a railway historian and author living north of Saigon.

Indeed, the conflict and railway are as closely linked as track and train. You can't mention one without the other, and in the centre of Hanoi sits another squat yellow building. As I walk towards Hoa Lo Prison, the humidity and high sun slow-cooks me in my own juices until I'm a gravy of sweat and sunscreen. Prisoners incarcerated here during the Vietnam War nicknamed it the "Hanoi Hilton", mocking the appalling living conditions. At its peak, 3,600 captives were squeezed into a space made for 300. I wander the shadowy corridors, noticing the iron bars in the envelope-sized windows that had been strained apart by desperate fingers. And in the confinement cells, the floor set at an angle so shackled prisoners couldn't lie back without the blood rushing to their head. Oedema and scabies were rampant.

After the war, the North–South line was a fragmented mass of twisted steel. An estimated 1,334 bridges, 158 stations and 27 tunnels had to be repaired and yet – just 20 months later – a train left Hanoi on 6 December 1976 and arrived in Saigon a month later to great fanfare as a symbol of Vietnamese unity.

That night we board the train, the bagpipe-style horn signalling our departure. I sit on the slim couchette as the carriages snail through the city, catching glimpses of residents in their evening routines. A young man admiring his new cut in the hairdresser's mirror, an old lady watching TV in her bed, and a barrage of bikes – their headlights bright as moons – waiting to cross the tracks.

I seek out Mr Tien and find him lying on the bottom bunk. He offers me a seat on the bed opposite and, with the train rocking rhythmically beneath us, tells me his story. "I was seventeen when I joined the war. Eight of my friends and I cut our fingers and made a blood pact to sign up early. It made the local radio – our families were so proud." He looks out the window and starts to smile at a memory. "You had to weigh forty-five kilos to pass the medical, but I was only forty-three kilos, so I put stones in my pockets!

"We were part of the anti-aircraft unit defending crossroads and T-junctions of the Ho Chi Minh Trail from American planes," he continues. "We had no huts, only hammocks, and the food was terrible. We could only hunt with traps because gunfire might reveal our location. We foraged for mushrooms, but it was dangerous – they'd often leave us vomiting. We'd have to eat fish floating dead in the river – we had no choice."

"What killed the fish?" I ask.

"The Agent Orange. I don't know why they called it that – it was white. It was a herbicide they used to decimate the forests. Every time we saw helicopters we ran away, against the wind, as fast as possible with handkerchiefs over our mouths. It would make us cough and scratch. A few days later all the leaves would fall off and the fish in the stream died. It was really hard, really difficult." Mr Tien pauses. "More died of malaria than bombs. That's why I went to St Petersburg after the war to study the parasite. We would call from hammock to hammock in the morning, waiting with dread if there was no answer."

"Did your friends all make it?" I ask, quietly.

"Three of us came back," he replied, staring at the floor and stroking his nose as if comforting himself. "At night, I still dream of burying my friends in the forest. We hoped their families could find the place after the war, but the bombs obliterated everything."

We sit in silence for a long while. "How do you feel about Americans now?" I venture.

"When American journalists came to conduct interviews at the end of the war I saw we had both been victims. I realise now it was a stupid war – completely avoidable." I return to my cabin and lie, eyes open, in the dark, comforted by the swaying.

When American B-52 bombers obliterated the bridges, stations and tracks, there was little point in rebuilding, so the 5,000 engineers sent from China to reanimate supply lines built "ghost bridges" at night (dismantling the tracks and hiding them during the day), or pontoons on the backs of boats strung together.

I awake as we're nearing Huê to see farmers manoeuvring their water buffalo through rice paddies and pops of pink lotus flowers floating in the ponds. Wafting through town is the coffee-coloured Perfume River – so-called because scented flowers from the forest fall into it as it runs westwards to Laos. Riverboats with snarling dragon heads ply tourists downstream, selling cheap magnets, kimonos and chopsticks. But away from the shimmer of polyester and plastic, are glimpses of real life. A boatman dredging the alluvial build-up has hung his laundry to dry on deck and I can see his wife washing up in the cabin. And on the roof of our own boat I find a small altar of yellow flowers and lit incense curling into the sticky sky.

On the northern bank sits Thien Mu Pagoda, a seven-tier seventeenth-century Buddhist tower flanked by frangipani trees and purple boughs of jacaranda. The scene is serene, but 50 years prior it was the site of Buddhist hunger strikes and protests in response to the discrimination they faced from Catholic President Ngô Đình Diêm. Parked at the back, is the Austin Westminster sedan in which Buddhist monk Thích Quang Đúc was driven to his self-immolation in Saigon on 11 June 1963. Its aqua-blue paint too flashy for the man of quiet resolve it carried.

We return to the rail station bound for the beach-resort city of Nha Trang, 400 miles to the south. A female guard sits in her office passing the time by sewing patterns onto a conical palm-leaf hat with fuchsia thread, while young men, their trousers lank around their skinny legs, wash the waiting carriages with soggy mops.

The ten-hour stretch is considered the most scenic section of the route, tunnelling through the Annamite Range and hugging the sandy half-moon bays of the Pacific Ocean coastline. I cautiously nose my head out of the half-open window between carriages, the wind raking my hair, to see thickets of white trumpet flowers trailing down to the sapphire shallows where the wooden rings of prawn farms stand sentinel.

Before long, the lunch cart trundles through proffering skewers of meat and whole deep-fried songbirds (head and scrawny wings intact). A fellow traveller dips into their wallet and hands the seller a few *dong*. "Dip them in the salt," he advises, handing over one of the crispy birds. Locals lean into the aisles to see what the verdict is as the traveller bites into the head and winces as the eyeballs pop.

As the hours pass, the carriage quiets as we're rocked briskly back and forth as if being peppered onto the tracks. Occasionally, a baby cockroach scuttles across the windowsill and a rumbling snore escapes the lips of the man behind me. At each stop, ladies board the train hawking clear plastic sacks of boiled eggs, rice cakes and jackfruit; leaping off when the alarm sounds.

En route to the canteen, I meet Thiều Pham Manh – captain of carriage number five – lazing on his side in the porters' cabin, sipping green tea. He waves me into the little nook and we sit cross-legged on the low bed. As he pours me a thimble-size cup, I notice the calluses on his feet and his tobacco-stained teeth. He's travelled the North–South route – four days on, four days off – for 24 years, he tells me, pointing to his home-made sign stuck on the corridor wall that reads: "Here to help", with his mobile number, trustingly, penned below. We share family photos on our phones, but hit a language barrier, so he dials his 18-year-old daughter Ky Dieu to translate over the phone, and our triad chat continues until the shadow of Nha Trang's high-rises emerges across the water.

I steer away from the city's world-class beach towards the local market. Beneath the high roof, the air hums with high-pitched bartering and the heady pong of fish. Smashed palm leaves litter the wet floor where eels, octopus and frogs writhe in buckets and bags. Women seated on their haunches cleaver the legs off blue crabs with a clean "thwack-thwack".

But the rails are calling for the final leg to Saigon. Everyone settles quickly and sits chuckling at the *Tom and Jerry* cartoons being screened in the aisle. A father and son sitting opposite me tuck into their packed lunch of rice and boiled eggs. Stormy rains lash the windows and sodden passengers clamber aboard gratefully at each stop. The father and son fall asleep, mouths agape. I wend towards the second-class coaches, passing men squatted between carriages smoking and snoozing kids coiled up on raffia mats splayed across the floor. Here, the seats are wooden and a bucket is propped beneath the air conditioning to catch the drips.

A young girl smiles shyly and motions for me to sit next to her. Her name is Thao Nguyên and she's returning to university. "I go home every weekend to help my father at our durian farm," she says. "My friends take the bus, but the is train cheaper – plus, its much better than five years ago when there was no air con or TV and the windows were jammed open so you'd be covered in dirt," she adds, turning to take in the scenery. Flooded rice paddies shine like shattered mirrors and rack-of-ribs cows graze the fields. I ask about the differences between the north and south. "People from the south always tease that people from Hanoi are so stingy they'd even steal the railway lines to sell," she says, holding her hands over her mouth to hide her giggle.

The streets of Saigon are awash. Shopkeepers huddle under awnings, ladling steaming pho into bowls and handing over cups of rocket-fuel coffee to power locals through the day. With railway tunnels echoing in our memory, we drive to a different kind – the Cù Chi Tunnels used by the Vietcong during the war. What started as private underground shelters to protect soldiers from arrest, grew into a network spanning 250 kilometres. Conscripted farmers-turned-fighters were often forced to spend up to a month in the tunnels during attacks. Shuffling through spaces 60 centimetres high and 50 centimetres wide and infested with poisonous spiders, snakes, millipedes and – worst of all – malarial mosquitos.

Their combat methods ranged from ingenious – such as issuing car-tyre shoes with the tread reversed so the enemy thought they were travelling in the opposite direction, to using water buffalo to pull the railway lines off-track, and training wasps to attack the smell of Americans – to brutal, with bamboo-spiked pits named the Clipping Armpit or the Folding Chair.

Lined up behind glass in the gift shop are an array of grenades and AK-47s. "'During the war, I used this one," says Mr Tien, matter-of-factly, pointing to a handheld grenade launcher, and catching us all off guard. Entering the forest of acacia and eucalyptus, the screech of cicadas is outmatched only by the unnerving crack of gunfire from tourists who have paid 500,000 *dong* (£20) to practice firing an AK-47 in the nearby range.

Here at Ben Dinh, sections of the tunnel have been reconstructed and our khaki-dressed guide, Thuân, leads us into the dark earth. It's almost double the height and width of the original structures, but my knees are tucked right into my chest. After ten minutes, my calves and hunched back are burning; my lungs tight from the breathless air. "My parents fought in these tunnels," explains Thuân. "They don't talk about it much." They, like the rest of Vietnam, are putting the past behind them. Like a train on tracks, the only way is forward.

And change is indeed afoot for the railway route. The wooden benches will be phased out by 2021 in favour of plush green seats, and the government is planning to adopt high-speed train technology to reduce the travel time. "Cockroaches will probably still be a regular feature, though," jokes historian Tim. But speeding up isn't always the answer. If time heals all wounds, the Reunification Express has – and continues to – provide just that. Hours at a stretch, when life is put on pause as the local landscape spools by. Creating time for a dad to talk to his son. Time for a university student to daydream without interruption. Time for a writer to drink tea with a carriage manager and, not once, talk of war.

CHANGE IN A SINGLE BREATH

———

Lilly Ryzebol *with* **Andrew Ryzebol**

For *Sidetracked* magazine
June 2019

I breathed deeply, from my stomach, calming myself, focusing my thoughts on my faith, my appreciation of the natural world, and my gratitude for life. Andrew floated beside me, in the hole he had cut in the ice. I drew comfort from his words: "OK, Lil, whenever you're ready." I took one final breath, removed my snorkel, and dove down into the dark other-worldly depths of Lake Huron's Georgian Bay.

My heart raced as I floated downwards. Beneath me, the eerie shadow of a shipwreck, shimmering as the light caught its warped bow. Above and around me an endless sheet of ice, pale blue against the darkness of the sea. Icy water seeped through my wetsuit and trickled down my spine. I shivered. All was quiet, tranquil and still. I felt small compared to the glacial leviathan that almost cocooned me. I breathed more slowly, lowering my heart rate and welcoming the calmness that would enable me to explore this magical sculpture, carved by ice and time. All with a single breath.

I lost both my parents to cancer at the age of 25. When my mother passed away, it changed my life completely. The prospect of losing her had terrified me, but when the day finally came I was supported by my faith and belief. Perhaps it was because of that grief, and the way I dealt with it, that I chose to face another fear that has dominated my life – being in water. When I was three years old, I almost drowned in a pool during a family trip to Indonesia. It was our last family vacation before my father's first cancer surgery. My uncle hauled me out of the water and resuscitated me. This led to a fear of being in water that has plagued me ever since. Whenever I found myself on a boat, or near a body of water, I became hesitant and afraid to even look down into the deep. I avoided pool parties and water sports, and was ashamed that I couldn't swim. The sound of waves crashing on rocks or the surf rushing on to a beach paralysed me. Yet I suddenly felt excited by the prospect of embarking on something new and unknown. Fear became fuel; a motivation to conquer a phobia that had held me back for far too long.

In early 2017, a good friend of mine, a scuba diver, on realising that I wanted to learn how to dive, recommended me to a local dive shop. After my first scuba-diving session I was hooked. Everything I had suffered, fear and grief, just dissolved underwater. I felt rejuvenated; confused, yet overjoyed. In truth, I felt alive. The dive instructors encouraged me to explore more and dive deeper. Fear of water evolved into a hunger for extreme underwater adventure. Over the next few months I took weekend courses including an introduction to freediving. I learned how to extend my breath-hold underwater without breathing apparatus. Each time I walked into the classroom, emotion flooded me – doubt, fear, excitement, nervousness all intertwined – but even more so during that first freediving class with my diving instructor, Andrew Ryzebol. Two of my great passions began in that class.

I became hooked on freediving. Fear became fascination. I trained in the pool four times a week and seized every opportunity to go diving. I held my breath everywhere I went to build CO_2 tolerance and did O_2 training tables whenever the opportunity arose. Freediving gave me peace. It helped me grieve, took me to places I could never have imagined, and offered me a sense of belonging and community. I explored shipwrecks and caves and reached depths I hadn't thought possible on a single breath. Once winter fell, many divers remained strictly in the pool or travelled south to warmer waters to train. Instead, Andrew introduced me to the world of ice diving. This type of diving presented greater challenges that improved my technique and built mental and physical resilience. Ice diving became the next hurdle to be overcome – in that environment, it is even more critical to be aware of your body and know your limits. Handling extreme cold, adjusting to erratic weather patterns, and maintaining good spacial awareness are all fundamental. There is only one entry and exit strategy: that tiny hole in the ice. I recall ice diving with Andrew and a friend of his, Geoff Combs. It was −20°C with ferocious 50 km/h wind. Snow slashed my face. As the boys chopped the ice hole with their axes, excitement, wonder, and fear eddied inside me. I thought to myself, "I'm crazy. What am I doing here? Why am I standing in the middle of a frozen lake, considering diving through a tiny hole in the ice? On a single breath?" After that dive, it all made sense.

The tranquillity below the surface soon overshadows the initial pain and discomfort. As I dive I close my eyes and focus on equalising my ears and gently kicking my fins to go deeper. As I kick down my senses are overwhelmed, my emotions heady and intense. I feel peace, wonder, mystery, cold, and a hint of apprehension all interlaced, coiling into something lyrical and beautiful. The silence is complete. Sanctuary from the drone of the city, the voice of my worries, and the ache of my grief. Once I was close to the bottom I opened my eyes to look up. A vast expanse of ice formed in sharp layers, varying in shapes and patterns everywhere I looked. Amazing, startling, breathtaking. Being 10 m below a ceiling of ice can induce fear and panic for those not properly prepared. But for me, it brought a new perspective on how wondrous nature is. Even in the most hostile environments, I found beauty.

One of the main attractions of diving on Lake Huron's Bruce Peninsula are the shipwrecks. This past season, Andrew and I dove beneath the ice and explored the Sweepstakes shipwreck – an old

119-ft two-mast wooden schooner built in 1867. The uncanny sensation that comes from diving beside a piece of history is something I will not soon forget. A silent ghost in the cold stillness, sinister and melancholy. Despite the site only being 20 ft deep, I was shocked at how many emotions came to me. Peace, wonder, fear, melancholy, joy – all are subsumed together into this one experience; all lead to a new perspective on life. These are the intrinsic pleasures of freediving.

Freediving has allowed me to go to places I had never before imagined. Diving shipwrecks, icebergs, and caves; swimming alongside sharks, manatees, whale sharks, stingrays, turtles, giant crabs, and octopuses. With a single breath, freediving has changed my life. I overcame lifelong fear and began to explore a deeper, richer side of my mind. The discipline and accomplishment inherent in ice diving have brought new purpose and meaning to my life and I have been blessed to witness the awe of creation. With the freedom I have found, the possibilities are endless.

THE OLD COUNTRY

Karen Edwards

For *High Life* magazine
November 2019

It is Wednesday morning in the Upper Hunza Valley and, in the small village of Gulmit, Sher Ali is working on his farm. Crouching among the rows of potato crops, he pulls out several bunches of weeds and tosses them into the yellow sack beside him. In the distance, wispy candyfloss clouds have settled around the snow-dusted Karakoram peaks, and the sun is gloriously full in the sky. It is quiet, except for the occasional revving of a tractor trudging up the hill. "This whole field is mine," Ali says proudly, gesturing to the vast paddock that surrounds us. "I grow potato, wheat and barley – the three staples. This place puts food on my family's table and…" he pauses and taps the side of his head, "it keeps my brain sharp."

I try to guess at Ali's age. His friendly face is lined with experience and his warm eyes slacken slightly when he smiles. He is dressed traditionally in a loose cotton *shalweer kameez*, a cooling outfit for working in the hot sun, and a flat cap. Yet I get the impression Ali's demeanour is misleading. This is a man who prides himself on his mental and physical strength and has the sense of humour to match.

Pulling out stubborn weeds with his bare hands, three or four stems at a time, Ali looks up at me with twinkling eyes. "I am seventy-eight years old but I am strong," he laughs. "My wife and I have been married for many years, but I had my first baby – a daughter – at sixty." He laughs again. "I told you, my body is very strong."

Like many other men of his generation, Ali moved to Lahore, one of Pakistan's three big cities, as a young man to "get a good job to support the family" by working in a textile mill. As a manager, his role was to ensure the quality of production. He returned to Gulmit decades later with savings, which he would not have collected had he stayed in Hunza, and a lifetime of experiences to share. You might think 40-odd years of work in a textile mill would mean Ali would be eager to put his feet up but, as his cracked fingertips and muddy nails show, he has other ideas. "Here, my body feels good," he tells me. "Anyway, I do not feel old enough to stop working. Even now I don't think of myself as an adult."

It might sound strange from a 78-year-old man, but Ali's way of thinking isn't unique here. In fact, there is a deep-rooted belief that *real* adulthood only comes with life experience, explains Salah Uddin, a 54-year-old Hunza-born culture specialist and tour guide for Wild Frontiers. "In other places adulthood is when we reach sexual maturity," he says. "But wisdom, adulthood, comes at maybe fifty or sixty years old."

Lucky then, that Hunza people tend to defy Pakistan's national life expectancy average of 67 years old, with villagers often living to see 100. While official statistics don't exist, many people speak of the centenarians among them.

Uddin says their philosophy unites the Hunza community and "encourages the younger generation to listen to elders' stories" – particularly the lessons learned from societal conflicts and hardships. The passing down of stories through generations brings a tremendous respect for those who have gone before and paved the way for a modern way of life. It also takes the pressure off young people to have all the answers, meaning there is space and time for the folly of youth.

In nearby Aliabad, the commercial centre of the Hunza District, Ibadat Shah, 96, agrees: "Working with the British Indian army, I went into communities and listened to elders speak about their experiences, both good and bad," he tells me. "Through them I learnt about the history of our people and how our society had evolved. It was only at around fifty years old that I felt I finally understood life. Now I share these stories with my children and grandchildren."

Farming is the leading industry in Aliabad, but as is now a rite of passage, the younger generation tend to go to the cities to make good money in higher-paid jobs. Just as in Gulmit, they return once retired to invest hard-earned savings in family farms and the modern concrete houses being built along the town's leafy lanes. Thanks to those who bring home savings, this is a prospering community.

At nearly 2,500 metres above sea level, the Hunza Valley is located in the northeast of Gilgit-Baltistan, Pakistan's northernmost territory – a spectacular region home to some of the world's most famous, and highest, mountain ranges. This is where the western Himalayas, Hindu Kush and Karakorams meet and it is as stunning as you would imagine. Still, few foreign tourists have experienced this beauty in the last 20 years.

While occasional militant upheaval does still occur, Pakistan – and Hunza – remains safe and welcoming for travellers. Earlier this year, prime minister and former cricketer, Imran Khan, introduced the online e-visa scheme, allowing easy entry for citizens of the UK and Europe. In June, British Airways reinstated its flight route from London to Islamabad after an 11-year break. This is a place where snow-covered summits provide the backdrop of almost every northern village. Rickety wooden suspension bridges cross the Hunza and Gilgit Rivers, linking villages to the winding Karakoram Highway mountain pass, an 810-mile stretch of road built to connect Pakistan's southern states to its northern region. Old mud and stone houses still dot the hills, alongside lush farms or cherry and apricot orchards. This is the time to experience Pakistan's unique rural culture, before the modern world takes over.

According to The Global Wellness Institute, wellness-related tourism grew by "6.5 per cent between 2015 and 2017, more than twice as fast as tourism overall". In the same period, well-being-oriented travellers spent 53 per cent more on trips than regular overseas tourists. In the West we continue to search for a mindful, healthy way of living, yet here in Pakistan this has been an accepted way of life for decades, and it comes without the hefty pricing and marketing jargon.

It is within the grounds of an orchard that I meet Shah and his wife Rasheeda Begum, 89. Both still work here and at their nearby farm where they harvest wheat and barley – as well as keeping cows and sheep. In the orchard, endless leafy trees bearing cherries shelter us from the hot sun; the scent of sweet, ripened fruit filling the air. After seven children, 15 grandchildren and two great-grandchildren later, they show no signs of retiring.

"We wake up at four a.m. every day to serve as volunteers at the local Ismaili Prayer Centre," says Begum, as she leads me by hand to a table on her veranda and piles several bunches of cherries onto a waiting plate. "After the prayers, we work on the farm. Our dedication to our work has looked after us." Her jolly face lights up as she slips into the role of grandmother, placing three cherries in my palm. "These are the tastiest cherries in Hunza," she winks.

Begum walks with a stick but is in good health. "In my younger years I was at home with seven small children as my husband was away working for the British Indian Army. I would look after our farm – often carrying more than forty kilos of produce, plus a small child, home – an hour's walk – every day."

"Our food is clean here," adds Shah, looking not one bit his 96 years. His skin is taut and his complexion glowing. "We do not put chemicals on our crops. Our vegetables are not processed or modified. Our food comes directly from the farm and onto our tables."

With her husband fast approaching a century, Begum attributes their longevity to "contentment". "Growing up there was no stress, no jealousy," she says. "Nowadays people are under pressure to make money, to be rich or famous. There is always something that brings stress." While modern amenities including smartphones have arrived in Gilgit-Baltistan, the emphasis on community welfare remains.

Shah nods in agreement. "Life used to be peaceful. We had good relationships with each other. If one family had less food one week, others would share their produce with them. In our community everyone is equal".

And with that, Shah leaves me pondering how, perhaps, a good life doesn't simply come from looking after ourselves – but also from looking out for each other. In the West we campaign for self-love, mindfulness and leading an active lifestyle, but perhaps it's time we recognised that our overall success as individuals comes down to the well-being of our society as a whole. Something the Hunza people seemed to have nailed, without pricy retreats, inspiring hashtags or snappy social media slogans.

"Our children are well and happy," Begum tells me with a beaming smile. "There's nothing more we can hope for – except perhaps for a peaceful world. We still wish for a peaceful world."

The Old Country
Photography by Kevin Faingnaert

The Night Train
Photography by Emily Garthwaite

Change in a Single Breath
Photography by Geoff Coombs

Long Walk to Freedom

Photography by Emily Garthwaite

Pirogue: Descent of the River Lulua, DRC

Photography by Archie Leeming

THE SECRETS OF HUNZA HAPPINESS

Sher Ali, 78: "Working in the field keeps you thinking on your feet and your mind sharp. It is when you stop working that your mind starts to go. It's good to be educated, but more importantly, be a good human being."

Rasheeda Begum, 89: "Be content with what you have. We need to learn to be less greedy, help those who have less than us and leave behind the things that cause stress."

Ibadat Ali, 96: "Be open to change. Hunza used to be very isolated – we lived in mud houses and had no facilities. Now we have tiles, floors, concrete houses – and we learned about these from developed cities. It is important to adapt."

TIM ZAGAT'S
GOURMET TOUR

Douglas Rogers

For *The Telegraph*
April 2008

Tim Zagat was missing. Somewhere between the reception and the private dining room of Thomas Keller's imperious Per Se restaurant in New York's Time Warner Center, the founder-publisher of the Zagat Survey restaurant guides had disappeared. I'd been warned about this kind of behaviour.

"You do realise," Michael Mahle, Zagat's communications director, had whispered as we set off on a five-hour "dine around" with his boss of the ten best restaurants in New York, "that with Tim anything can happen?"

There are few more pleasurable – or unpredictable – experiences than visiting the city's best restaurants with the man who knows them better than anyone. A dashing 66-year-old, with a rasping bourbon-and-cigar-soaked voice and meaty 6-ft-2-in, 250-lb frame (testament to three decades of dining out), Tim Zagat is the Orson Welles of the New York restaurant world; a man with a manic enthusiasm for good food and good times that would exhaust a teenager.

What I hadn't expected was that he would stray off menu so soon. It was only 6.45 p.m. and we had nine other restaurants to see – kitchens to tour, master chefs to meet, sushi and steak to sample – and already the worry was we'd never make it out of Per Se.

"He's through there," said a busboy ferrying imported Hawaiian Hearts of Peach Palm into Per Se's $30-million, 5,400-sq-ft kitchen.

We headed off down a long, ceramic-tiled corridor, past a wall-mounted television screen beaming live footage of French Laundry, Keller's Napa Valley restaurant. All around was a hushed, focused intensity that was more science lab than restaurant: chefs were delicately drizzling Russian caviar over plates of iced oysters; wrapping smoked bacon around sirloins of farm rabbit.

Before it opened in 2004, waiters at Per Se took dance classes to learn to serve with added grace. That television screen? It was so that the cooks could keep in tune with their counterparts in the French Laundry kitchen.

Eventually we tracked Zagat down to the confectionery room. He was flirting with two pastry chefs, handing out free subscriptions to his online guide, and helping himself to packets of freshly baked coconut truffles.

It was in 1977 that Zagat and his wife, Nina, both Yale-educated Manhattan lawyers, started collecting reviews of New York restaurants written by dinner party friends. They hit upon an idea: why not produce a restaurant guide written by ordinary diners instead of food critics?

The democratic formula paid off: today Zagat is a vast publishing empire, with restaurant surveys covering 60 cities around the world, as well as guides to nightclubs, spas, hotels, golf courses and food markets. More than 300,000 people vote in the surveys, their opinions are condensed into quotable review form by hundreds of editorial staff at the Zagat offices overlooking the Time Warner Center on Central Park.

But while the distinctive purple-red dining guide is an institution – the "Burgundy Bible" as New Yorkers call it – Tim Zagat's tours of restaurants, his "dine arounds", are the stuff of legend. He visits more than 600 New York restaurants a year, and as part of his rounds will often invite friends and journalists along for the ride. Zagat eats dinner out five nights a week and lunch most days.

My own plan was simple: to visit the ten best restaurants as listed in the 2008 guide, and eat dinner with Tim and Nina (who would join us later), in the last of them. Mahle had drawn up our itinerary and would ride shotgun to keep us as much on schedule as humanly possible.

Our second official stop was Jean-Georges, the Columbus Circle restaurant of Jean-Georges Vongerichten in the lobby of the Trump Hotel. The seas part when Zagat walks into a restaurant. Receptionists flutter their eyes, maître d's trip over themselves to offer their best tables, and those who don't recognise him soon step into line. "I'm Tim Zagat," he'll say, holding up a copy of his book. "I do this."

Still, I was surprised to find Vongerichten himself waiting at the front desk to give me a tour of his café and fine-dining restaurant. In the kitchen I sampled a freshly baked cinnamon marshmallow petit four that comes with an espresso order; it evaporated in my mouth like a magical sweet foam. "Room service," Jean-Georges smiled. Guests at Trump's hotel get the food of the sixth-finest restaurant in New York sent to their rooms.

Two French restaurants have vied for the top Zagat rating for the past five years: Daniel, on the Upper East Side; and the seafood restaurant Le Bernadin on West 51st Street. Le Bernadin was next, and we hopped into a chauffeur-driven town car and headed south.

The genius of Zagat's guide – at least for Zagat – is that although he doesn't write the reviews, restaurants still fawn over him as if he did. However, he never accepts complimentary meals, and when a team of waiters at Le Bernadin scurried round offering wine and champagne, he ordered water and made sure Mahle paid for it. "I try not to drink on a tour until the end," he said. "Otherwise, I'd get stuck in one place."

I didn't have the same problem and tossed back a pricey glass of burgundy while chef/owner Eric Ripert, a friend of Zagat, guided us through an elegant dining room lined with nineteenth-century French paintings and past a private upstairs salon where 40 Japanese bankers were cutting deals over plates of sea-urchin caviar and escolar with miso butter.

Le Bernadin slipped to third in this year's Zagat ratings, but Ripert seemed unfazed. He reminded Zagat to come to the party he was hosting the next night for the launch of *My Last Supper: 50 Great Chefs and Their Final Meals*, at which Ripert (who is on the book's cover), was to roast a Puerto Rican whole hog and administer a whippet shot of truffle foam to the mouths of the guests. "Must I?" Zagat grins. "I hate this job!"

When we arrived in the Four Seasons Hotel lobby to visit the jewel-box-sized L'Atelier de Joël Robuchon (ranked 10th), a dapper gent in a tailored suit and pink tie greeted him warmly as we walked past. "That was Peter Browne," Zagat shrugged (Peter Browne as in assistant to the Beatles and namechecked in John Lennon's *Ballad of John and Yoko*: "Peter Browne called to say 'You can make it OK, you can get married in Gibraltar near Spain'.")

Most of Zagat's energy comes from an insatiable love of food. Arriving outside Sushi Seki, a cult Japanese hole-in-the-wall in the Upper East Side, rated ninth in Zagat, his car door lightly bumped a cyclist ferrying a Chinese food delivery. Zagat apologised, and then his eyes lit up: "What you got there? Noodles? Mmm... smells good."

There are 2,069 restaurants in the 2008 guide, but as we drove around Zagat would tell the driver to stop if he saw an establishment he'd not been in before; then he'd run in with pad and pen to make notes.

"Go into a restaurant and you can tell if it's good without eating in it," he explained. "I look at the people inside, the menu, the kitchen – it has to have a liveliness, an animation." He paused. "I tell you what, if you really want to know great New York restaurants you really should meet Sirio. Driver, take us to Le Cirque!" And we veered deliciously off course again.

Le Cirque is not in the Zagat top ten, but it's one of the most famous restaurants on earth.

Opened in 1974 by Tuscan-born Sirio Maccioni – "the world's great maître d' and owner," said Zagat – it's been a gourmet playground for global high society for 30 years. It recently moved to the sleek glass-and-steel Bloomberg tower on East 58th Street, where, incredibly, Maccioni, 76 and a cross between Don Corleone and Marcello Mastroianni in his black tux and dark glasses, still greets his guests at the front door. He gave Zagat a hug and was soon gliding me through a sumptuous circular dining room set below a billowing silk circus tent, the walls a shiny, lacquered ebony.

We'd just missed Nancy Reagan and Henry Kissinger, but the banker Sandy Weill was at one table and the scent of money and power in there was as strong as the smell of black truffles on the plates of foie-gras ravioli.

Adjacent to the bar, Zagat showed me a wall of photographs of Maccioni with friends: Sinatra, Jackie O, Sophia Loren, Bill Clinton, Silvio Berlusconi. The story goes that Pope John Paul II once asked if he could reserve a table at Le Cirque. Maccioni told him: "Of course, but can you guarantee me a table in heaven?"

"My ambition," Zagat said dreamily, "is to make it up on this wall!"

Le Cirque is not all about celebrity. Maccioni popularised such dishes as crème brûlée and pasta primavera, and helped launch the careers of master chefs Daniel Boulud and David Bouley, whose eponymous restaurants are rated one and seven respectively in Zagat.

It was way past 10 p.m. now and it was clear we were not going to make it to Peter Luger, the Brooklyn steakhouse, nor to Chanterelle, the French classic of David and Karen Waltuck in Tribeca. Mahle called Nina to say we'd be dining at Bouley in Tribeca, but first we'd see two more restaurants uptown: Daniel and Sushi Yasuda. And it was there, inevitably, that the wheels came off.

In Daniel, a haute-Renaissance palace of red velvet carpets, Venetian pillars and coiffed Upper East Side sophisticates dining on frogs legs and foie gras and milk-fed pig, I ordered a basil-infused vodka cocktail at a gorgeous gold-leafed bar counter to survey the glamorous scene. Zagat, forgetting his no-booze rule, asked me for a sip – and then downed the whole drink. He turned to Mahle who also had a cocktail. "Come on, Michael," he growled – and downed his drink too. "Right," he said, "anyone for sushi?"

Sushi Yasuda was 22 blocks south. I'd never heard of it, but it's the highest-rated Asian restaurant in Zagat's history. It was on the ground floor of a nondescript commercial block on East 43rd Street. The décor is unremarkable – blond wood, bright light – but the dozen tables were heaving, and behind the counter Naomichi Yasuda, a big, bald Japanese chef in his fifties, was rolling rice and cutting fish with the flourishing precision of an orchestra maestro. When he saw Zagat walk in three stools miraculously became available at the counter. "Mr Zagat," he smiled. "Sit. Sit. I take care of you…"

It started with Long Island Spanish mackerel paired with a sake served on a miniature bamboo mat. Then a portion of Idaho rainbow trout with a different drink. Florida eel came next, spiced up with a rare, rich shot of soy sauce. A piece of Rhode Island bonito went down, smooth as an oyster. Each portion of fish was paired with a sake from a different Japanese region, which we swiftly knocked back. Then came an extraordinary, sloppy, pungent sea urchin from Santa Barbara. "Best aphrodisiac in world," said Yasuda.

Mahle briefly popped out to call Nina to tell her we were running late. While he was out, Zagat ate his portion of Hamachi yellowtail. "Don't tell him," he ordered – then ate his own. I asked the young couple next to me how they chose the restaurant. "We found it in Zagat," the woman said. Zagat heard her and winked. "It's a great book, isn't it?" Then he drank more sake and another tuna slice. "You wouldn't think we have reservations at Bouley tonight, would you?" he grinned. "Hey, do you want to come with us?"

I suspect they might have, except it was then that Nina marched in. A soft-spoken brunette, she had the definite air of someone who had seen her husband in action many times before. She suggested it might be best we call it a night before her husband created more havoc. Zagat's schoolboy grin briefly gave way to disappointment; it was clear who wore the trousers around here, he would have to go home.

Mahle ordered me a cab while I watched Nina shove Zagat into the back of the town car. As it sped away, he managed to stick his head out the window. "Go to Bouley!" he commanded me. "It's brilliant!" And then they were gone, off to their Upper West Side apartment overlooking Central Park. It was way past 1 a.m.

LET THERE
BE LIGHT

Amelia Duggan

For *National Geographic Traveller*
April 2019

Night in the African bush falls like a portcullis. Dusk is a leisurely curtain call of deep reds and glowing umber but then, as if a switch were flicked, the light exits stage west, sucking every drop of colour with it.

It's in this sudden blackness that I'm left blinking and shivering despite the heat, standing alone on the flat roof of a solitary cabin in the middle of Majete Game Reserve, watching the headlights of the 4×4 that just dropped me off disappear into the night.

The cabin is an outpost of the luxurious Mkulumadzi Lodge some miles away. There's a king-size bed in the centre of the rooftop, enclosed in a giant teardrop of mosquito net. I patrol around it, dim lantern in one hand and emergency horn clutched in the other, trying to make sense of the primordial darkness. Gradually, shadowy masses around the hut untangle into distinct outlines of gnarled mopane trees and the limbs of euphorbia cacti curling skywards like candelabra. I try to identify unfamiliar noises: the rush of a river barrelling southwards from Lake Malawi; the beating wings of bats overhead; the crackle of creatures moving through the desiccated undergrowth. For the first time in a safari park, I pray the Big Five stay well away.

Above me, a shooting star drops lazily through the heavens. This is the spectacle I've been left here to enjoy: from horizon to horizon, the firmament is ablaze. It's spellbinding. I feel like I'm on the edge of the earth looking into the cosmos. The Milky Way arcs over the bed. The low crescent moon is a glowing stud in my starry headboard. Planets twinkle distinctly. It's as if I've got my own, incredibly colourful orrery: there's the topaz glow of Mercury, the diamond of Venus, the ruby of Mars. I switch off the lantern and let the starlight brighten. And this is how I spend my first night in Malawi: watched over by the planets and stars, and wrapped up in the heavy cloak of a benign, wild spring night. It's magical.

Sticking it out alone on an experience usually offered to couples has the unintended consequence of impressing my safari guide, Mustafa. "You didn't get scared? I thought for sure you'd call us back!" he laughs as we take morning tea in the bush besides the Mkulumadzi River. Mustafa radiates goodwill and chuckles like it's going out of fashion. They don't call the country "The Warm Heart of Africa" for nothing. The natural kingdom, in particular, provides a constant source of joy for him. And it's infectious. Driving earlier that morning through tall forests, where quartz boulders shimmer like disco balls, we shared gleeful squeals at scuttling warthogs, uproarious belly laughs at rutting impala, and giggles of astonishment at a herd of elephants.

We kick off our boots and paddle in the shallows, just another pair of animals out for a cooling dip. The sandy bank was decorated overnight by countless paws, hooves and talons – a testament to the thriving ecosystem that's been painstakingly nurtured back to health from an out-and-out poaching crisis. I spot the large impressions of elephant feet; the sand has perfectly preserved the cracks in its skin, which appear like raised tributaries on a map. A park ranger, Ado, wearing a smart navy-blue uniform and carrying a very powerful .458-calibre rifle, stands sentry on the shore. "I feel so proud of what we've achieved here," he tells me later in an unguarded moment as we hike to see the confluence of the Shire and Mkulumadzi Rivers. We watch the two raging currents, each with its own colour and texture, smash into each other and vie for dominance as gravity pulls them downstream. "Things could have gone another way entirely."

Before African Parks took over the administration of Majete in 2003, poaching had decimated the park. The non-profit organisation has a reputation for rejuvenating floundering parks (including four in Malawi alone) to the benefit of local communities, but with only a handful of antelope remaining inside Majete's 270-sq-mile perimeter, and tourism all but dead, the odds here were stacked. Gradually, however, relations with the surrounding villages were improved; rangers like Ado were given military-style training; and Africa's most iconic animals were successfully reintroduced. Rhinos and elephants at first, and then a dozen more species including leopards and lions. For a country once known for being among the world's least-developed, it's a fantastic success story that's seen it become a conservation leader in Africa. Now, Majete is Malawi's first, and so far only, Big Five park – a responsibility Ado takes seriously: "We've never lost a single rhino or elephant to poaching, not in fifteen years. Things are changing in Malawi."

A few days later I head to Liwonde National Park, which has recently been given a second chance, too. "We have orange snow at the moment," Steegan, the manager of Kuthengo Camp, observes with a note of apology when I step off the jetty and accept an iced tea from her under the billowing boughs of a fever tree. Odd, spherical flower puffs eddy around us, caught in the breeze. Bushbuck graze at the river's edge. The peace is broken only by bird cries. Somehow, amid all this beauty, I'm the only guest. Kuthengo (meaning "in the bush" in the national language of Chichewa) became Liwonde's second safari operation when it opened in 2018 with a handful of luxury tents smack bang on the fertile Shire floodplain. "It's pronounced 'Shir-ree,'" head guide, Stanley, corrects me gently as we head back out on the water for safari.

Chugging along the placid Shire with swallows flitting around our boat and the sunlight flickering behind borassus palms, it's hard to imagine Liwonde in disharmony. Stanley details the mammoth restoration projects undertaken since African Parks assumed management in 2015. One was to dig out 36,000 wire poaching snares. Another was to tackle elephant overpopulation, which conservationists achieved in a historic feat by tranquillising and relocating 336 to a reserve in the country's north.

From the boat, views span across reeds dotted with birds as bright as baubles and long-legged waders stalking the shallows. "As many as a thousand crocodiles live in every mile of this river," Stanley says, with a warning look to the hand I've got trailing in the water. Hippos snort disgruntled greetings as we pass, twiddling their terracotta ears and eying the boat with unconcealed menace. We spot elephants on the shoreline – around 60 of them, with calves – breaking from the treeline and heading our way for a drink. Zebras, too, among the tall grass, and reedbuck and waterbuck and sable, all with young. There's new life everywhere.

The Shire River was dubbed "God's highway" by Scottish explorer and missionary Dr David Livingstone when he reached these parts in 1859. He was searching for a river route that could open up the heart of Africa; but discovered to his disappointment that, as the Shire flows out of Lake Malawi towards the Zambezi in Mozambique, it drops 1,300 ft through a series of impassable falls. Stanley takes me to see the park's oldest baobab tree where Livingstone pitched camp. It's a vast cathedral of a tree with a hollow trunk, buttressed on one side by the knitted branches of an equally ancient fig tree.

We climb inside the tree, standing where Livingstone once stood. His expedition, during which he "discovered" Lake Malawi, ushered in colonialism: Britain staked a claim to Nyasaland, as Malawi was called, in 1891. After achieving full independence in 1964, the country stagnated for three decades under the dictatorship of Hastings Banda. Malawi's eventual return to democracy in 1994 did little to elevate its reputation: until very recently, regional instability and economic turmoil put tourists off. It's a relief to climb out of the dark baobab and be reminded of how much brighter the future is looking.

For my last few nights in the park, I move to Mvuu Lodge, which for 25 years was the only camp in the whole of Liwonde. It's there I meet a guide, David, who promises to introduce me to the park's newest residents: lions, released in 2018, and cheetahs, reintroduced the year before. "The impala didn't get a vote on it," he jokes darkly. The park is focused on restoring poached-out populations, with wild dog and giraffe next on the list, and David tells me tourism is slowly increasing as travellers like me come to witness the revival.

We set off early, before dawn has broken, but still need to move fast and cover a lot of ground if we're going to catch a big cat out hunting. David hangs out of the side of the vehicle while driving, scouring the dirt for tracks, but it's the circling vultures that give us our first lead. We approach and find the carcass of an impala being plucked apart by scavengers. "It's moved on. But it must be close."

David's right: as we round a thorny thicket decorated with the nests of weaver birds, I catch sight of something red among the yellow and dun of the plain. My brain is still scrambling to interpret the scene when David slams on the brakes. It's a cheetah with a fresh kill. It releases the bushbuck's neck from its blood-spattered jaws and stares at us. I see the distinctive black tear lines on its face, its neat spots, the creamy fur on its belly, the way it blends in with its surroundings. "We just missed the action!" David laments, spotting the rest of the bushbuck herd cantering away. Still, when you consider that before this cheetah's arrival, Malawi had been completely devoid of the predator for 20 years, we're here at just the right time.

RARE SPECIES

Driving south-east on dusty roads, dodging goats and people, mud-brick villages built on parched red earth peter out and the terrain rises into lush electric-green tea plantations. In the heart of these highlands, on the slopes of Mount Thyolo, there exists a rare monument to the grandeur – and pioneering spirit – of Malawi's colonial era. As with the national parks, at Satemwa Tea Estate there's a move to salvage Malawi's natural and cultural riches for posterity.

"There was a storm last night and it's taking some time for the power to come back," Tracy, the manager of Huntingdon House, explains as we tour the manor built by Maclean Kay at the heart of the plantation. "All part of the pioneering experience!" she adds cheerily. It's dusk, and the housekeeper is lighting tall candles in the dining room. Light glints on the polished Edwardian furniture and mahogany bookshelves and catches the silverware on the tables. Through large windows that open on to a veranda set with armchairs, children are playing croquet on a lawn. Tracy straightens a painting on the wall, and for a moment this could be an old country house in Britain. But then a gecko shoots up the wall from behind it. "Let me introduce you to our bats," she suggests casually, leading me through a maze of doors to stand under the eaves of a secret patio. "They're a rare species."

The romantic manor, wrapped in vines and creepers, has been a central character in the Kay family saga since its construction in 1935. It was here that Chip Kay, Maclean's now-elderly son, grew up and raised his own family. In 2009, in a move to share Malawi's colonial heritage with the public, five bedrooms were opened up to guests. It's full of charming quirks: a honeymoon suite in a chapel ("never consecrated", Tracy assures me); roll-top tubs where bubble baths come with a dose of borehole silt; and a Wi-Fi connection best experienced with a drink and plenty of patience. With his handlebar moustache, Chip himself is one of Huntingdon's historic attractions – another rare breed in these parts – but his poor health keeps me from hearing his legendary stories.

So instead of the past, I look to the present and the future of Satemwa. In the morning, a wild breeze blows up from the tea terraces, over the manicured beds of dusky hydrangeas and explores the house, troubling the drapes and tugging on my sleeve to get outside and explore. Around 10,000 rolling acres of tea and coffee and blue gum trees await. On a sweaty mountain bike ride, I discover the joys of eating coffee beans straight from the bush and of drinking tea on the factory floor with the tasters. I stop and chat with a group of female pickers wearing traditional chitenje (patterned cloth) wrap skirts, who find my presence so alien and entertaining that work is halted to indulge in a rib-splitting fit of giggles.

Huntingdon may have its roots in a sophisticated era of silver-service suppers and sundowners, but it's also a place to hitch-hike up dirt tracks in the back of a pickup to picnic spots, or to get your hands grubby. Besides exporting coffees and teas around the world and investing in the lives of its 1,500 workers, Satemwa is committed to restoring Malawi's forests, which are shrinking as a result of unregulated farming. This is why I find myself wielding a rustic hoe for an afternoon, digging ditches then smoothing the earth around mahogany saplings. Nothing but warm smiles greet me as I traipse red clods of earth across Huntingdon's hearth.

LAKE OF STARS

If my first week set me up with an impression of pristine landscapes and a sense of a country emerging lighter and more hopeful from a weighty past, then it's down at the lake shore that I come face to face with the energy of modern Malawi. The annual Lake of Stars Festival is back after a hiatus, and down on the beach I'm dancing barefoot to live bands among a mix of fashionable urbanites from Blantyre and Lilongwe, local beach bums and aid workers on furlough. "This is the biggest party anywhere in Africa right now!" the lead singer of a Kenyan boy band yells to a crowd of thousands. Behind the main stage, upstaging all the acts, Lake Malawi stretches to the horizon.

This is landlocked Malawi's greatest treasure. Measuring 360 miles north to south, and filling a deep trench of the Great Rift Valley, Lake Malawi is one of the planet's most fascinating freshwater ecosystems. Hundreds of unique fish species call it home, and the water is so clear and calm that sometimes it feels like swimming in an aquarium. It's an absorbing masterpiece of vivid hues that's positively hypnotic, especially at sunset when the waves shimmer gold and pink.

When the festival wraps up and the crowds disperse, I follow the shore south to the sucrose beaches of Cape Maclear in Lake Malawi National Park. It's the type of easy-going paradise that ensnares wandering backpackers: lazy days become lazy weeks, whiled away in lakefront bars learning strategies of the board game bao or browsing village stalls for carved souvenirs. "No one seems to use time here," I overhear a new arrival say. "It's only 'yesterday', 'today' or 'tomorrow'." But I can't linger: I still have my eye on the horizon.

Early the next morning, I board an antique fishing boat in Cape Maclear. It chugs slowly out into the lake until the mainland becomes a hazy shimmer and a tiny rocky island rears into view. Below its crown of trees are five thatched bamboo cabins, set above a cove and scattered among colossal boulders. This is Mumbo Island, an off-grid eco-camp at the heart of the national park and, as luck would have it, I'm the only guest again. I throw myself into the role of Robinson Crusoe. I take a kayak out and circle the island, spotting otters among the rocks, then tip myself overboard to snorkel through a kaleidoscope of cichlid fish. In the cool of late afternoon, I follow a treasure map through the island's sun-dappled woodlands to find secret caves and viewpoints and then, as the sun sinks, I sit on the island's sandy beach, which is empty except for a pair of large, lazing monitor lizards.

That night, I struggle to sleep, and when I step out onto the deck of my cabin for some fresh air, I have to rub my eyes. There are distant pinpricks of light on the surface of the dark lake, as if entire constellations have fallen from the night sky into the water and continued to blaze. I realise it's the same scene Dr Livingstone saw when he visited in 1859; the reason he described it as the "lake of stars". Each orb is a fisherman working by the glow of a lantern hung from the prow of their boat, the way they've done for centuries. I curl up in my hammock and enjoy the moment, suspended between the ancient lights of the heavens and their twinkling echoes on the water. And this is how I spend my last night in Malawi, much like I did my first: alone in the wilderness, surrounded by stars.

THE HAJJ DIARIES

Tharik Hussain

For *Lonely Planet* magazine
August 2019

THE ARRIVAL AND THE HARDSHIP

"If you ask a hundred people what this means to them, everyone will say something different to you," said Sheikh Suleiman as he pushed my aunt's wheelchair. Born in Uganda and educated in Madinah, our guide for the Hajj was a tall, handsome man with a warm smile. When he walked it was with the kind of grace and dignity I had seen earlier in the stride of tall Nigerians and in the shuffle of the older Yemenis as they circled the Ka'aba. Our group of six Hajjis – two in wheelchairs – were the second group the Sheikh had led through the *umrah* rituals that day, each one taking nearly four hours. It was a wonderful privilege to have him all to ourselves and now, as we headed out of the world's largest mosque, he wanted to know what the Hajj meant to me.

There were many meanings, I said, but one of the most beautiful is the unity. Living in England, I was used to being around people from all over the world, but here, I explained, I felt a special connection to the broad-shouldered Afghan thumbing his *tasbiyyah* (prayer beads); I understood why the tears flowed from the eyes of the wispy-bearded Indonesian; and I too wanted the *niqab*-wearing Saudi woman's prayers to be answered. The pinnacle and most visually striking example of this unity is the *tawaf* – an essential feature of the Hajj – where seemingly disparate individuals move in unison as one around the symbol of God's oneness, the Ka'aba.

There are three ways most people perform the Hajj; *Qiraan, Thamattu* and *Ifraad*. We were performing Hajj *Thamattu*, which meant entering a state of purity, *ihram*, first to complete *umrah*, then coming out of it for a few days, and then again assuming *ihram* ahead of the Hajj proper, on the eighth day of the Islamic month of Dhu'l Hijjah.

Our journey thus far had been a surprisingly smooth one. Despite an industrial strike at London's Heathrow airport threatening chaos, we arrived to find our flight on schedule and a terminal so quiet it was eerie. Check-in and security took less than an hour. The Hajjis in our group, including my mother, saw this as divine intervention. "It's the quietest I've ever known it," said Tristan, a Heathrow assistant from Goa, India, sensing my amazement. The serenity followed us onto the plane.

Apart from one individual who forgot to bring his two white sheets into the cabin to assume *ihram* onboard — the eventual rescue by someone carrying a spare set was also attributed to a higher power — the flight passed with little incident. Once the pilot announced we were flying over the station for assuming *ihram,* the cabin, now filled with men wearing only two white sheets, and women in their chosen attire, made their intentions and began loudly announcing (in Arabic) their arrival — the *talbiyah*: "Here I am! O Allah! Here I am at Your service! Here I am at Your service," we chanted in rhythmic unison over and over again.

Our small family group consisted of my mother, my aunt (her twin) and her son, Rafique. Our mothers were already Hajjis and were performing these in lieu of those that had passed on. My mother was doing the Hajj for their late father, and my aunt, for her late son. As we left the plane to board the shuttle buses in the relative cool of the Saudi night, both of them reminded us of the many hours they had spent standing in the scorching desert sun with our fathers at this very airport the last time they were here. We all wondered what awaited us this time.

The bus pulled up at a terminal even emptier than the one at Heathrow. Entering the cool air-conditioned immigration area, a Saudi wearing a red-and-white *keffiya* and *igal* bowed and said, "Assalamu alaikum, welcome to Saudi Arabia." I wondered if we were in the wrong place.

With only passengers from our plane making up the queues, the necessary pictures and thumbprints took almost no time and soon we found ourselves in an equally relaxed arrivals hall. Men in white sheets meandered past towards the terminal's mosque to pray in congregation, others queued politely to exchange money, and some headed for a coffee bar. No one had lost their luggage – just a wheelchair momentarily – we had all been treated with dignity and respect at immigration. A mere two hours after stepping off Saudi Air flight SV112, we were watching the bright lights of Jeddah disappear behind us as our coach turned on to the highway leading to Islam's holiest city.

We had experienced none of the horrors of arriving in Saudi Arabia during the Hajj that are legend in almost every Muslim family and it all felt rather surreal. My mother and the Hajjis again saw divine intervention.

Tomorrow, we leave for the pilgrimage proper when we'll be camping in the mountains surrounding Makkah to engage in ancient rituals. In doing so, we will experience another meaning of the Hajj: connecting with the great prophets, from Muhammad, through Ibrahim, all the way back to Adam and Eve. However, this will be done alongside an estimated 2.5 million Hajjis, creating yet another great display of the Hajj's famous oneness, and another meaning for the Hajj, one I hadn't yet experienced when the Sheikh questioned me: hardship.

THE HAJJ PROPER

The Abdul Aziz Bridge was full of men wrapped in white sheets taking in the awesome views of the tent city of Mina, the colour of their *ihram* outfits matching the sea of identical snow-white cones sprawled out below us. Hemmed in on all sides by steep hills of granite, the tents were punctuated only by the sand-coloured minarets of the Masjid al Kuwaiti.

It was past the mid-afternoon *asr* prayer and the heat of the day had begun to subside. Having entered the state of purity again and arrived in Mina in the dead of the night chanting the *talbiyah*, the Hajj proper had started for us. Most Hajjis had then spent the morning in *ibada* (worship) inside the cramped and congested tents, and now many had come out to stretch their legs.

Some were on phones updating loved ones, others photographed themselves against the iconic tent backdrop, but most simply stood and stared, lost in their thoughts. Behind them, the last of the coaches ferrying people from Makkah to Mina roared past. They would be back soon to repeat the feat three more times, taking the hajjis to Arafat then Muzdalifah and finally back to Makkah – the equivalent of moving the entire population of Namibia to four different spots over the course of five days.

Mina is where the Hajjis come to contemplate, worship and rest, just as Muhammad had done in the seventh century, ahead of the most important day of the Hajj.

"Being at Arafat on the ninth of Dhu'l Hijjah is the only act of the Hajj that cannot be missed. If you do, you will have to come back next year to perform the Hajj again," our Sheikh had reminded us.

Any other act of the Hajj could be missed and compensated through various "fines" – mostly involving feeding the poor – but missing the day of Arafat was not an option.

The poor were at the forefront of my thoughts as I made my way down from the bridge into the forecourt of the Kuwaiti mosque. Hundreds of unofficial hajjis had pitched up here. African and Asian women sat on reed mats, nursing children and eating pre-prepared travel meals. In another age, they would be cooking their meals here, but that was banned after a fire in 1997 – started by exploding cooking-gas canisters – killed around 200 people.

The sky was now turning a delicious pinkish red. I tiptoed around resting hajjis, past an amputee using shoe heels to protect his knee stubs, to sit on a set of clean stairs near the *wudu* area. The air was filled with the waft of liver being fried with onions and peppers in one of the eateries behind us. Next to me sat a heavily moustached Pakistani man staring out towards the sculpted skyline of the mountains beyond the mosque. I followed his gaze and together we watched the birds dancing about them.

"My name is Abid, I'm a banker from Islamabad," he said, after I introduced myself. "I've come alone. The children are too young for this. And you?"

As I began telling Abid bhai (honorific "brother") my story, the *adhan* for the sunset prayer began, stirring Hajjis from their impromptu naps. They stood up and shook off their rugs before shuffling over to the *wudu* queue which quickly doubled in length.

Abid bhai led me to a spot beside the stairs, where a Hajji offered us his place to pray. We smiled and thanked him before standing in silence ahead of the *iqama* (call to start the prayer).

Abid bhai spoke perfect English and was clearly an educated man. His soft, manicured skin told me he had lived a good life. When we departed, he gave me an intense hug, one that seemed to carry much sadness, and when it was finished, Abid bhai said nothing. Maybe he couldn't. He just cupped his hands together and looked skyward. He wanted me to pray for him and I nodded, promising I would.

That night, as I lay in a tent in camp 41a atop fold-up brown foam "beds", inches from Hajjis either side of me, I thought of Abid bhai again, along with all the others I had promised to remember on the Day of Arafat, now mere hours away.

Centred around Jebel ar Rahma — the Mountain of Mercy — Arafat is where us Hajjis would assemble tomorrow as a reminder of the Last Assembly (judgement day), a place where every request made by the Hajji on the 9th of Dhu'l Hijja is said to be granted.

Knowing this I had given friends and family the opportunity to privately send me their "requests", promising to deliver them in person. I wrote down every request I received: an exercise that truly humbled me. People had been extremely candid and trusting, and the requests left my own list looking a lot less urgent.

I added Abid bhai to the list and began running through some of the others in my head as I lay there in the dark, only the sound of the industrial air-conditioning vents and the occasional cough breaking the silence.

I was again reminded of just how privileged and blessed I really was. I didn't have to pray for any of my children's health, nor that of a parent; my mother was in the tent next door, my marriage wasn't on the rocks and no traumatic disaster had befallen me. In fact, barring the request for the safe and healthy birth of my third child, I decided if there was a queuing system, I would be happy for God to put my requests at the back of it.

When I eventually drifted off, I managed to close my eyes for no more than an hour before I was roused by the urgent and loud call of: "Wake up, brothers. It's *fajr* time!"

Bleary-eyed and disorientated, we made our way to the camp's shambolic toilet and shower facilities to wash and prepare for the sunrise prayer and the day of reckoning. Soon the buses would arrive to ferry all of us to the plain of Arafat. Our first day of the Hajj was over, but the main one was just about to start.

THE DAY OF RECKONING

The grating "scrunch-scrunch" of a million squashed plastic bottles beneath our sandals was making it difficult to focus. I held my mother's hand tight to stop her slipping.

Around us, 100 *talbiyahs* were being chanted by the Hajjis slowly shuffling towards the focal point of the plain of Arafat, the Mountain of Mercy.

It was late afternoon; an earlier thunderstorm had cooled the temperature considerably and thinned out the crowds. This had given me the confidence to take my mother to visit the revered mountain.

Arafat was where Adam and Eve had been forgiven by God, and in AD 632, on this very day, it was where the Prophet Muhammad had completed his mission whilst performing his own Hajj.

During his one and only pilgrimage, the Prophet laid out the non-negotiable rite of being in Arafat on the 9th of Dhu'l Hijjah until the setting of the sun – he had said nothing about being at the mountain.

The sheer volume trying to visit it earlier was the reason Rafique and I had left our mothers praying in their tent, and with two fellow Hajjis in tow, joined the huge mass of pilgrims, moving glacier-like, towards Jebel Ar Rahma. Using umbrellas to keep the midday sun off our heads, few noticed the dark, foreboding clouds gathering in the distance.

By the time the granite face of the mountain came into view – awash with the white *ihram* of pilgrims atop it – a large crack overhead was followed by a strong wind sweeping through the valley, turning our cheap brollies inside out and leaving us exposed to the imminent downpour.

The unexpected opening of the heavens on the most auspicious day of the Hajj aroused joyous shouts of "Allahu Akbar" – God is great – all around us; the Hajjis saw it as a sign of God's bounty. According to tradition, rain in the desert is nothing short of a miracle, laden with blessings.

Up ahead, the thick crowd near the foot of the stairwell leading up the mountain was slowly coming to a standstill, and the soldiers charged with controlling the flow reacted quickly by diverting Hajjis – us included – away from the mountain.

This annoyed some pilgrims who broke away to scramble up the slippery, jagged rock face; having patiently shuffled along for the last hour to reach the mountain, they were not about to be denied. Those of us watching observed another miracle, as somehow no one slipped and caused themselves serious injury.

Eventually, we also broke away, to find a spot near the mount.

The four of us stood, eyes closed, arms outstretched, facing Makkah; lost in our own individual supplications, completely oblivious to everything around us.

The rain streamed down our faces, mixing with salty tears; I tried to recall the individual requests people had asked me to remember. As I said each person's name slowly and deliberately in my head, the voices outside began to fade to a whisper. By the time I moved on to my personal supplications, I could hear nothing except my own pleadings.

It was a powerful moment. The moment we had come to the Hajj for.

Now, at a turn in the road where Bangladeshi migrant workers in green boiler suits haplessly held out plastic bin bags, I tried to recall the names I had forgotten to mention earlier. My mother handed me a few Saudi riyal notes, and I discreetly placed them in the top pockets of the workers as we passed them. They smiled and nodded in acknowledgement.

At the foot of the mount, I guided my mother to a space beside a group of Arab women, one of whom was wearing a traditional thin, metal face mask. Above us, the mount was still awash with the white of men's *ihrams,* but now the atmosphere had changed. People sensed time was running out. Soon the sun would set on this blessed window, when it is said any request made by a Hajji standing on the plain is granted. The murmur of 1,000 incantations being rapidly whispered cascaded down the rock face.

My mother and I spent the next 30 minutes making sure we maximised our opportunity. As she made supplications for a Hajj dedicated to her father, I did my best to recall the requests I had forgotten the first time.

On our way back to our tent, she pointed out the trees lining the route.

"You see those? They're called 'Zia' trees," she said with pride. "They're named after former Bangladesh president Ziaur Rahman. When he came for Hajj, he saw how scorched the plain was and told the King of Saudi that the Neem tree of Bangladesh provided excellent shade and he would send some saplings to be planted here to shade future Hajjis. In return, the Saudi King promised to accept more Bangladeshi workers into his kingdom."

I wasn't sure about the veracity of the story, but listened with a smile. There aren't many tales about Bangladeshi workers in Saudi Arabia that make people smile, so I was glad to hear this one.

General Ziaur Rahman was the second President of Bangladesh, and the man who declared the country's independence on 27 March 1971 by radio. My mother would've been an 18-year-old bride with a one-year-old babe in arms. The previous day the War of Independence had begun, which would see almost 3 million Bangladeshis killed.

That evening, I stood atop a large rock looming over the plain of Muzdalifah, our third destination for the day. Before me, a vast ocean of sleeping bodies stretched out as far as the eye could see. It was like nothing I had ever witnessed before.

Somehow, before the day was done, the Hajj authorities had managed to get all of us to this thin stretch of desert for our third rite of the pilgrimage. Now we were to pray, collect pebbles for the stoning ritual tomorrow, and bed down, out in the open with nothing between us and the starry desert sky.

THE DEVIL WITHIN

All over the world, Muslims were celebrating Eid, but not us.

The 10th of Dhu'l Hijjah doesn't feel like Eid for pilgrims. It is the day I had been dreading more than any other – the day we were to perform the *jamarāt*. In recent years, as numbers attending the Hajj have continued to grow, this has been the deadliest of rites.

"I was standing near the Great Column thinking: so this is how it feels to be crushed. I no longer knew where my body ended and the masses began, and much like everyone else around me, I started to panic," wrote Bulgarian-German Ilija Trojanow about his *jamarāt* experience in 2003. At least 18 Hajjis were trampled to death there that year. A year later, in 2004, a further 250 died in a stampede at a *jamarāt* bridge; this was followed by 345 Hajjis perishing in a crush in 2006. But the worst tragedy in Hajj history happened a mere four years ago. The Associated Press reported that over 2,400 pilgrims died in a deadly collision at a *jamarāt* bridge in 2015.

Trojanow's book was one of the pilgrim accounts I had read en route to the Hajj, and now as we moved, snail-pace, inside a giant concrete tunnel with tens of thousands of other pilgrims – the ominous sound of ventilation high above – I was filled with a sense of genuine foreboding. My mother shuffled along beside me, reciting and holding her sister's hand. Rafique was pushing her wheelchair, closely followed by our friend Moni pushing his mother. Every so often, the leader of a large group shouted out the *talbiyyah*:

"*Labbayk Allahumma Labbayk!*"

"*LABBAYK ALLAHUMMA LABBAYK!*" roared back the pilgrims.

This was punctuated by the Saudi soldiers, stationed at regular intervals, screaming "*Yallah Hajji, Yallah, Yallah!*" every time a pilgrim tried to stop or turn back to look for someone.

An aggressive chain of Hajjis, linked at elbows, pushed their way through, inducing glares from everyone. After a number of gruelling days with very little sleep and the onset of the infamous "Hajj Flu", patience and politeness was in low supply. According to

Islamic tradition, the three pillars stand on the spots where the devil had tried to tempt the prophet Abraham on three separate occasions. Each time he did, Abraham had responded by pelting him with seven small stones.

Our symbolic re-enactment of this was meant to affirm our own rejection of temptation. After an hour or so, the August sunshine appeared like a bright light at the end of the tunnel. Up ahead, the *jamarāt* resembled a giant multistorey car park, spread over five floors. We were heading to the third, where mercifully the path opened up into a wide covered hall, thinning the crowds.

Outside, several equally claustrophobia-inducing streams of white pilgrims could be seen moving slowly along broad, raised bridges, each leading on to a different floor. Ahead of us three gargantuan walls – replacing the old pillars – sat in huge concrete funnels. The clever design offered Hajjis wider targets, and they were able to spread themselves along the length of the walls. Once the pebbles hit these, they ricocheted down through the funnels to the very spots where the ancient pillars had once stood.

It was the first of the three obligatory days of *jamarāt*, so we ignored walls one and two, and made straight for the third one – over the next two days we would stone all three.

Hurrying past the first swell of Hajjis, I led my mother to the far end of the wall, followed closely by Rafique and Moni. The two of them were ushered into an area cordoned off for the exclusive use of wheelchairs, and we slipped into a gap behind them.

Standing face to face with the large concrete facade, the two of us threw our pebbles one by one, repeating the words "*Allahu akbar*". Within minutes we were done, slipping out and away from the growing crowd, into a clearing where we stood and faced the direction of the Ka'aba to make our supplications.

Rafique and Moni soon joined us with their mothers, and before I knew it, we were all on the road to Makkah again. The whole affair could not have gone smoother and was a far cry from poor Trojanow's traumatic experience, all those years ago. As we joined the crowds of people streaming towards the holy city, I was filled with an immense sense of relief. We had broken the back of the Hajj, without incident, and soon we would perform the *tawaaf al-ilfaadah*, confirm the Eid sacrifice had been made on our behalf (at the Hajj slaughterhouses), and shave our heads to exit the state of *ihram*. The hardest part of the Hajj was done.

Over the next two days, we returned to Mina in a more relaxed state. Dressed in our normal clothes, we left our mothers in the safety of the tents to perform the remainder of the stoning ceremonies for ourselves and on their behalf. Finally on the 13th of Dhu'l Hijjah, we made our way back to Makkah. The only real trial during this period were the Mina conditions, which caused several Hajjis to fall ill. The swirl of air conditioning inside the congested tents and the awful bathrooms were prime bacteria breeding grounds. Few of us could get our heads around why the Hajj authorities expected us to defecate in the same place we were to shower.

"This is how things like cholera begin," our Sheikh had said to me, as I wondered out loud who thought it was a good idea to install the showerhead in the toilet cubicle.

The Hajj authorities had clearly worked hard to improve many facilities, the *jamarāt* complex and the efficiency of transfer between sites amongst the most impressive, but this was an obvious blind spot.

These were the things bothering me as I stared out at the uninspiring hotels of Aziziyah district, flashing past one last time, from the air-conditioned comfort of the Hajj authorities bus. Soon the green face of the Makkah clock tower came into view.

Seeing it, I slumped into my seat, feeling suddenly overwhelmed. Not from elation, as I might have expected, or even a sense of triumph. What I felt as I headed back to the revered Black House was relief.

We had done it. We had completed the Hajj.

UP IN ALMS

James Draven

For *National Geographic Traveller*
June 2019

Feet pad rhythmically through silent backstreets. Each individual step is scarcely audible, but together, in reverential unison, the crunch of gravel makes a sleeping stray dog's ear twitch and involuntarily turn towards our approach.

It's not yet 5 a.m. and this subdued, somnolent procession wends through desolate residential streets whose colours have been sapped into the void of the black sky above; lent sepia tones by the dim glow of road lamps. Nobody speaks.

I'm in Luang Prabang in Laos, walking silently with a small group of travellers each too tired to talk, only opening their mouths to yawn, to help keep open eyes glossed with tears of exhaustion. For many of us, a late night only ended an hour or two ago, and being pried from our beds at 4.30 a.m. has rendered us unable to communicate in any meaningful way. So instead we sleepwalk towards the centre of town, just as the faithful of Luang Prabang have done for hundreds of years.

The ancient practice of *tak bat* is woven into the fabric of Lao culture. This daily almsgiving ritual of Theravada Buddhism – which dates back at least 600 years – sees the townsfolk rise before dawn to cook batches of sticky rice, the daily bread for the town's monks, ready for reverential donation on the streets of Luang Prabang. In return, the monks bestow merit unto devotees – karma capital for the next life; the only currency you can take with you to the grave.

As we turn on to the arterial Sakkaline Road, the town is suddenly lively with groups of tourists, most of whom are being herded like sheep by umbrella-waving tour guides. Hawkers mingle with the crowds, carrying cigarette trays laden with candy bars and pre-packaged Rice Krispies Squares; overpriced offerings to those wanting the chance to buy a stairway to nirvana. The distant illuminated market-stall canopies, neon-lit stores and the fluorescent strip lights of food carts are diffused by a light, early morning mist, and the surrounding mountains are barely visible against the inky sky. Amid all this, on the pavement at the side of the road, locals kneel on roughly hewn mats, each with a big pot of rice before them.

I take my place beside them and put my own bowl of rice on the footpath in front of me. Then I kneel, pointing my feet behind me as tradition and respect dictates. My companions join me, a few of them buying packs of sweets to supplement their rice, and we wait.

As the sky pales from indigo to violet, faint peach robes appear amid the distant mist, darkening to saffron as the first of the monks comes into view. I hold my breath as they approach. Self-consciously – partly ashamed of my meagre offerings and slightly overawed by the spectacle – I reach into my woven basket and tear out a chunk of sticky rice, about half the size of a golf ball. It's glutinous and, well, sticky on my fingers. I drop it onto a young monk's plate and he looks at me with condescending approval. I guess I've earned my first merit point.

I'm so bemused by the experience that I miss the next two monks in line. Their silent, meditative, barefoot procession continues inexorably through town, past gilded temples and French colonial mansions shuttered with rich, dark wood, and past us, the faithful and tourist alike. It's an endless orange array of hundreds upon hundreds of monks. Soon, though, I find my rhythm, and I'm pulling clumps of rice from my pot and depositing them in begging bowls like an automaton. After a while, I realise I can no longer see where the line of monks ends and where it begins. A flip book of uniform, shaven-headed faces looks down on me approvingly as I mechanically dole out my scant offerings in a trance-like state to him, and him, and him, and him. The spell is broken, however, when a companion to my right places a Rice Krispies Square upon an alms-collecting plate.

For the first time I see a different expression in this cavalcade of faces: a quizzical look, a frown. I turn my head to follow the perplexed monk who continues to march with his peers, but whose reverie is temporarily broken as he turns the blue foil packet over in his hands and examines this incongruous rice offering. After a few more paces, he tosses it into a dustbin, then disappears, becoming invisible among his companions as his naked feet once again pad rhythmically in reverential unison.

THE LAND
OF *NO HAY*

J. R. Patterson

For *Overland Magazine*
November 2019

Advice is like bitter medicine. Even if it's good for us, we don't want to receive it. In all likelihood, if advice were a medicine, it would be a suppository. When travelling and beset by other travellers, I clench particularly tightly. How much trustworthy advice can you expect from a person with only a passing knowledge of where they've been? Certainly, it can make a remarkable difference by the time you find yourself there days or months later. But alongside a grain of salt, a fellow traveller's advice is still worth taking, even if it turns out to be a placebo, a worthless sugar pill of knowledge that only fooled you into thinking something. If nothing else, it acts as a reminder to keep a healthy observance.

When I encountered northbound travellers while motorcycling in South America, those who drove indicated that gasoline was impossible to come by in Bolivia. It wasn't that it was scarce. It was there, just not equally for everyone. There seemed to be little discrepancy in the advice. Anyone driving a vehicle registered to an *extranjero* (foreigner), could expect to pay two to three times the regular price for fuel, if they were serviced at all. The filling of jerrycans was meant to be illegal. The phrase *"no hay gasolina"* (there is no gasoline) passed from the lips of station attendants and was spread to motorcyclists from Buenos Aires to Bogota.

"It's the land of *no hay*," one rider told me before I went. "Even if there were something to get, you wouldn't find anyone that'd help you get it. Most indifferent place I've ever been."

This kind of indifference can seem like an affront to the traveller, particularly those astride a motorcycle. A motorcycle is a decidedly conspicuous way to travel, and even the most disillusioned riders can become accustomed to the fervour of passers-by and the interested crowds that gather around their machine. Being ignored, although a gift to those who wish to gaze into a culture unperturbed, can seem like an insult.

Impervious to this, and the issue of gasoline availability, were some of the faster riders, especially the Yukon-to-Tierra-del-Fuego-and-back-in-six-weeks types. Typically, they had nothing to say – they were hardly in any country long enough to notice local discrepancies and anyway, their 1,000-mile-range fuel tanks rarely warranted the need for checking in at backwater pumps.

Several theories for the fuel regulations were floated. Conspiracies involving embargos or corruption were common. A disdain for foreign travellers was another, and one of the more entertaining reasons. In a country where the exchange rate reduces most necessities to pennies, why *not* charge a little extra? There were tales of fuel thieves and the harsh punishments that befell them, and conflicting reports that either rural or urban stations were better. Occasionally and fortuitously, a travelling policy wonk would interject and note that Bolivian fuel was subsidised by the government but only for Bolivian nationals, didn't we know?

Still, the chatter over fuel made me slightly nervous. I knew from the highlands of Peru that Andean fuel stations could be hard to come by. With my '80 XJ650 only making 125 miles to the tank with a tailwind, I'd often come close to running dry.

The crossing into Bolivia at Desaguadero, unlike so many borders since Canada, was memorable only for being unmemorable. Despite sitting on the banks of Lake Titicaca, the town was parched, a droughty ghost town. Like the excavation its name implies (in Spanish, *desaguadero* means to slough off excess water), the town appeared bereft. Besides the cryptid presence of an efficient, smiling border guard (when had I ever encountered one of those?) and a few stooped women clawing at the ground with wicker brooms, there was no one about. Where were the loiterers, the money changers, the hang-abouts? It was less a town than a cold, flattened outpost on the altiplano. It was late morning and the high number of squat, boarded-up buildings added to the chilly air of abandonment. After unsuccessfully withdrawing cash from the town's ATM, I turned the last of my Peruvian soles into Bolivianos, bought a tasteless, dusty meal of fried meat and rice and, not wanting to linger, rode into the country.

The road unfurled peaceably toward La Paz, winding purposefully past fields of crouched men and women. Bundled in thick woollen sweaters, the women in bowler hats, their dresses like upended tulips, they looked ancient. Hacking at trapezoidal flaxen crops with hand scythes, they stacked the bound sheaves in pyramidal stooks, a sight so antiquated they would have caused my father to reminisce.

It wasn't long before I needed fuel. I had 25 Bolivianos, enough, I hoped, for an accommodating amount. I pulled into the first station I came to. Sidling up to the pump, I remembered the medicinal *no hay* warnings I'd swallowed. I made the gamble that, by keeping my helmet on, I could pull a fast one.

"Twenty-five Bolivianos' worth," I said to the attendant. She was fresh-faced and young but hadn't been born yesterday. After a quick glance around my bike, she shook her head. *"Extranjero,"* she said. *"No hay gasolina."*

I looked around. There was nothing but windswept, cookie-crumb emptiness. It was not a place I envisioned myself staying. I adopted a beseeching character and cited my non-existent desire to reach La Paz. When that failed, I appealed to her nationalism and mentioned fictitious Mennonite relatives living in the religious communities of Cochabamba. She only shook her head and pointed to a camera in the corner of the roof covering the pumps.

"Camera," she whispered. The trepidation in her voice told me there was no use in asking again. I rode on timidly, feathering everything, trying to conserve every ounce of remaining petrol until I nudged into the next station, shuddering with fuel starvation. The pumps were so similar, I wondered if I had somehow doubled back and returned to the fresh-faced young woman. But this fuel attendant had none of her contemporary's hesitation. Before I could ready my imploring speech, she had unlatched the nozzle and was in a position to pump. No questions, no eyeing my number plate, no *"no hay"*. I hurriedly unlocked my fuel tank, stammering "Only twenty-five worth!" With the satisfying tick of the pump as background, I scribbled in my notebook. Moments later, I looked up and realised in horror the price of the tank was nearing 50 Bolivianos.

"Stop!" I cried. The woman smiled confusingly and continued to pump while the numbers ticked up to 80. Exasperated and worried, I dug out my wallet and took out the few notes I had.

"I've only twenty-five," I said, holding up the tattered bills. I opened the wallet for effect, showing its empty folds. The attendant looked confused, then a familiar flash of fear shadowed her face. I thought of cameras, the laws that punish fuel thieves. Not knowing what to do, I thrust the notes into her hand, mumbled an apology and sped off.

It was some miles later, still burning with the thrill of escape, I saw the police. They came into view too late and I was pulled over. The charge was speeding (50 miles per hour in an urban zone), the fine 200 Bolivianos or approximately fifteen pounds. Not that it mattered – I still had no money. I told the policeman as much. He repeated this to his three partners who lounged against the hood of an SUV, and whose laugh suggested they had heard that particular phrase from every rich gringo who burned rubber through their speed trap. I laughed too, brought out my wallet and displayed its empty folds as I'd done at the petrol station, then stood up and turned out my moneyless pockets, the international symbol for "what the hell do you want now?" The officer gave another little laugh and called his partners over. After some miming and backslapping, the charge appeared to be dropped and I trundled on toward La Paz, scot-free. No penalty, no *hay castigo*.

———————————

Like most American countries, the foreign mistreatment of Bolivia's resources and people is older than the country itself. What are normally considered natural barriers to invasion – craggy snow-capped mountains, thick and humid jungle and wide, arid salt plains – have instead provided the very means of foreign exploitation. The Amazon is continually felled to make way for fields of soybeans, cotton and sugar cane. Foreign demand for a better battery and electric cars has spurred on plans to dredge more lithium from the Salar de Uyuni salt flat. Historically, Potosí's Cerro Rico, or rich hill, provided colonial Spain with its glut of silver, while Bolivia provided much of the raw labour in the form of *acémilas humasnasto*, or human mules, who excavated and processed the mineral before the Spaniards loaded it onto their treasure fleets. The mining continues to the present day, as does a queer sort of new-age exploitation – for a pittance, tour operators take tourists down into the working mines where they can buy coca for exhausted, soot-stained miners before detonating their own stick of dynamite.

A tendency toward signing away mineral rights and resource access to foreign firms in favour of short-lived gains has resulted in a centuries-long boom-and-bust national economy that hasn't slowed foreign interest in Bolivia's assets. Despite the constant extracting, felling and refining of its natural resources, Bolivia remains one of the poorest countries in the world, with 40 per cent of the population living in poverty. Through his Movement Toward Socialism, President Evo Morales has tried to reverse the effects of, as he says, "five hundred years of suffering", but it is an uphill battle. The primary building block of re-establishing the country's economy was to renationalise as many companies as possible. So it was that Yacimientos Petrolíferos Fiscales Bolivianos (YPFB), the company responsible for all aspects of oil and natural gas production, came under state ownership and began imposing levees on foreign drivers who crossed into Bolivia from Peru, Argentina and others, to take advantage of cheap rates. It was the new, public-minded Bolivia, quietly but adamantly asserting its rights in a bid to make up for lost time.

————————

For days after my roadside encounter with the police, I wondered if it was those special Bolivian qualities – friendly without being assertive, observant without being smothering, kind without expectation – which had made for their history of abuse. There was national pride, certainly – they had a varied history of starting wars and stringing up the odd president – but, just as I'd been warned, the people radiated an air of indifference. I began to worry that, if I needed help, I'd be on my own. Could it also be no help – *no hay ayuda?*

Thus turned away, I set out on the road from Potosí to Uyuni, a stretch of some 130 miles. There was no question of whether I'd make it. I set out with only a half tank from Potosí and the unusable instructions to "try the next place down the road" – according to my map, the next place was Uyuni. I went off anyway, too frustrated and proud to beg for fuel any longer.

Fifteen miles later I was descending into a wide valley on fumes. Rising up like a sculpted spoon's edge were barren orange and purple mountains. Across the valley, the thin ribbon of road rose up and zagged through a hidden pass. I knew I wouldn't have the fuel to make it that far, much less beyond the valley. But then, I spotted something. Camouflaged against the taupe moonscape of the valley floor was a grid of buildings. I felt elated, then, as I approached, crushed when I realised most of the buildings were a mess of crumbling mud brick and caved-in thatch work. I pulled in anyway, thinking I could catch a ride somewhere or, failing that, move into one of the houses.

Of all the buildings on the central plaza, only one had an open window, the top of a split-level Dutch door, beside which hung a grey chalkboard. Scribbled in a weak hand were the words *No Hay*. Something had been written underneath, then erased. *No hay nada* seemed to be the message. Looking into the darkness beyond the window, I could see the walls lined with empty shelving. When I knocked on the wooden door and called into the room, a small, pants-less child ran out from somewhere. Immediately behind him came a woman who scooped him up and held him protectively against her. She stood beyond the room and was bathed in light. Her clothes and face were dark brown, her crow-black hair pulled back tightly into a long braid.

"*Hola?*" I said, adding hopefully, "*Gasolina?*"

She shook her head and disappeared beyond my sight. I waited a moment, then returned to the motorcycle and sat on the pavement in the cold air and sunshine. I was completely unsure of what to do. The road was quiet, the town was empty. No one had appeared at the loud sound of my motorcycle. I wondered if they had hidden instead. I threw a few stones, trying to delay my decision. I was miles from anywhere, in a dusty town that wasn't even on the map.

Then, pushing her way through the door was the woman. She carried a gallon jug of petrol, a plastic funnel and a pair of pantyhose. Wordlessly, she placed them beside me then shuffled back into the store. I sat stupefied for a moment, then filled my tank, pouring the petrol through the pantyhose. Afterwards, I placed the items inside and called for the woman. There was no answer, no sound at all. Without complaint, without question, this Bolivian altruist had provided then sunk into obscurity.

Travellers sometimes forget that countries are for living, not visiting. Forget the bitter medicine, the illness was only skin-deep. Underneath the Bolivians' superficial indifference lay a strong compassion for those in need. While those who demanded may find none, others who waited would find help even in the unlikeliest of places. It was only a gallon of fuel, but it made all the difference. I tucked a wodge of notes under the jug. I knew I'd run into trouble again, but there was no doubt in my mind that I would find help. No question, *no hay pregunta*.

A GRITTY CITY COMING INTO ITS OWN

Noo Saro-Wiwa

For *Condé Nast Traveller*
December 2020

Switching from the slumber of Middle England to the sensory explosion that is Lagos was a transition I had to make during childhood summers. Life in Surrey was punctuated by returns to Nigeria where I was born, enforced by parents who were hell-bent on neutralising my Britishness. Reaching our home town of Port Harcourt involved stopping over at relatives' houses in Lagos, and even at that young age the big-city charge of the then-capital − its noise and swagger − was magnetic, repellent and always unforgettable.

The last time I took an extended trip here was in 2007, at the beginning of a four-and-a-half-month odyssey around the country for my book, *Looking for Transwonderland: Travels in Nigeria*. There was an organised chaos to it. I was intimidated by the density and impatience of the crowds and the kamikaze *okada* − motorcycle taxis − that flew at me from every direction. It was a steam pot of vehicle fumes and go-slow traffic jams which vendors weaved through, selling anything from squash rackets to books titled *How to Get Fat*, while self-styled preachers on the distinctive yellow danfo minibuses laid seven shades of Jesus on their fellow passengers. An urban jungle with the Darwinian survival ethos of Texas and the infrastructure of Kinshasa, where islands of staggering wealth existed without shame in a lake of poverty. If the state were a person, she would wear a Gucci jacket and a cheap hair weave, cruising in her Porsche over rain-flooded potholes. In a nation where the middle class had atrophied and the rich got rich very quickly, the poor were not irrational for believing that prosperity was within their reach. Nearly everyone had a side hustle, with even university lecturers supplementing their income by hawking Chinese cure-all teas on public transport. Rawness abounded.

A while later, I was preparing to fly back to the metropolis and found myself walking past *Vogue* writer Suzy Menkes in the airport. "Is this the departure gate for Lagos?" she asked me. Twenty years ago I might have assumed she meant Lagos in Portugal. Why would the grande dame of British fashion journalism be visiting African Lagos, whose notoriety strikes fear into the hearts of delicate First World travellers? It turned out Menkes was heading to Lagos Fashion Week, her presence proof that society is opening its eyes to Nigeria's largest city as a hub of design, art, industry and finance. But while its appeal is often overshadowed by infamy, it had been shining at the centre of its own universe long before the West began to take notice.

Recently, I returned to a Lagos that is better governed and more sedate in certain areas, a place with a vision of itself and where it wants to be. In prosperous neighbourhoods such as Victoria Island and Ikoyi, the *okada* have gone, replaced by *keke* – motorised tricycles – while the notorious yellow taxis now compete with Uber. One driver I encountered, Marcel, held a white-collar job at Guinness until he was laid off when the currency plummeted. Today, he uses his car to pay his bills and, compared to some yellow-taxi operators, he is intensely agreeable: the side hustle has been digitised, and the passenger-driver screaming matches of old are diplomatically muted now that both parties have app ratings to protect.

Marcel, like many Lagosians, isn't originally from here. Nigerians from all corners are sucked into the force field of a city which, if an independent country, would have the fifth-largest economy in Africa. Forty per cent of its residents are rumoured to be Igbo from the east – ironic considering it was the Igbos' attempt at secession that sparked the Biafran civil war of the late 1960s. My parents fled from that very conflict and settled in Lagos for a few years. Since then, it has grown to accommodate people from all of Nigeria's 200-plus ethnic groups who live in a phenomenal harmoniousness that is underappreciated by the world. "Lagos is Nigeria," one resident tells me.

Aesthetically, it wins no prizes. There are flashes of beauty in the university campus or the Third Mainland Bridge that snakes along the blue lagoon and sparkles in the twilight, but the panorama of seventies and eighties oil-boom buildings is as grey as the tropical thunderclouds, and the pavements are cleaved by open ditches. This is no place for the placid flâneur. Lagos's charm is concealed in its interiors, such as Alára, a gorgeous boutique by David Adjaye, the architect behind Washington, DC's National Museum of African American History and Culture. It may be set opposite a decrepit property in Victoria Island, but stepping inside I was dazzled by the imposing central staircase backed by huge windows with light pouring on leather goods and YSL clothes. "The city's an experiential space," says Alára's manager Hunderson, a shaven-headed Haitian New Yorker who has lived in Lagos since 2018. "It pulled me in. I didn't have a choice. When I first visited ten years ago, I thought, 'Oh my god, I can't go back!' The energy, the starkness... It's a blank canvas with about twenty-one million inhabitants. You can't be lazy. That's what drives me. Look at the fashion industry, the film industry – and everyone has a law degree. What is it with these people and law degrees?" he laughs.

October and November are the months to be in Lagos. The rains have ceased and the hotels teem with the local style set; Aké Arts and Book Festival draws the best writers from the continent and its diaspora, including Booker Prize winner Bernardine Evaristo and sci-fi talent Nnedi Okorafor. By night, the lagoon glows with open-air waterside bars and restaurants. And music is everywhere, the beats and electronic melismatic vocals of acts such as Burna Boy, who performed at Coachella last year, thumping from speakers. It can exhilarate or irritate, depending on your tastes.

I grab some respite at the Jazzhole bookstore, a long-time fixture on Awolowo Road in Ikoyi, an affluent central district where British expats built homes in the twentieth century. Here I sip coffee and scan the shelves while "Rhythm of Love" by seventies Nigerian funk band Blo plays in the background. Owner Kunle Tejuoso tells me his mother, Gbemi, used to run the family's other, now-defunct bookshop, Glendora, on the same street. My father would hang out there back in the day, perusing paperbacks and gisting (chatting) with Mrs Tejuoso. In a place where silence is a rarity, Jazzhole is still a good spot to meet new people and hold deep conversations. "This is not a city of the mind," one customer laments. It's true that designated intellectual spaces and events are thin on the ground, but sit in cafés and food joints and you'll overhear movers and shakers discussing the paucity of accurate cancer diagnostic equipment, or how low-cost housing subsidies end up benefiting the rich.

Here in the south-west, education levels are typically higher on average than in the rest of the country. One can see it in the home-grown tech companies of the Yaba neighbourhood, or Andela, a firm that aims to fix the global shortage of software developers. It makes the city's car-registration-plate motto, Centre of Excellence, look a lot less sarcastic these days. Lagos is Nigerian ambition made manifest, yet its predominant poverty is impossible to sidestep. To be an educated, cosmopolitan Lagosian is to be the world's consummate urbanite, because he or she experiences the full spectrum of the human condition. It keeps the empathetic ones grounded and inspired.

"We have so much raw material," says Tayo Ogunbiyi as we tuck into *obokun*, or saltwater catfish, at Switch 1922 Lounge in the Lekki district. She is the artistic director of Art X Lagos, West Africa's first international art fair. Philadelphia-raised and Princeton-educated, Ogunbiyi now lives here and helps to showcase exciting contemporary works from the continent and its diaspora. She says she needs the friction of the "real" Lagos to fuel her own creative works and remind her of what matters.

I agree. Victoria Island and Ikoyi may be packed with creature comforts – such as scoffing shrimp beside the pool at Moist Beach Club – but after kicking about among the suburban malls and nouveau-riche mansions hoisted by neoclassical columns, I'm craving the true urban no matter how gritty.

Onikan is a palate cleanser in that respect. Once the main downtown area, this district on Lagos Island has faded in looks and status yet still possesses the organic soul of the city. I like the worn apartment blocks with their exposed laundry lines, and the echoey acoustics of the cheek-by-jowl architecture. There's nearby Freedom Park, formerly Her Majesty's Broad Street Prison, with its pitted, late-Victorian walls within which public debates and concerts are held. On Bamgbose Street, a stretch filled with colourful multistorey houses, market stalls sell fruit and live chickens. Towards one end stands the Doherty Villa, one of the few remaining edifices built by the freed Brazilian slaves who settled here in the nineteenth century.

Over at dimly lit, old-school Ghana High Restaurant, office workers line up for typical Nigerian plates such as garri, a pounded cassava paste that is dipped into spicy soups made from groundnuts, leafy vegetables and okra. Hunks of grilled chicken and beef with jollof rice – a paella-style dish made from tomato stew, chilli and peppers – are served by a broad and imperious "madam" who doesn't bother with smiley customer service – her food is better than sex and she knows it.

Outside Tafawa Balewa Square, the cast-iron gates are topped by statues of eagles and giant white horses rearing towards the sky. There's a whiff of Mussolini in the design, but it is cancelled out by the vibrant umbrellas of the vendors below – vernacular street scenes that blend with the grandeur to unintentionally kitsch effect.

In Onikan I can see an opportunity for bottom-up regeneration. Hints of a brighter future are glimpsed in spots such as the Rele Gallery on Military Street, owned by Adenrele Sonariwo and displaying modern pieces by Nigerian artists including Victor Ehikhamenor. Down the road, in a park across from the national museum, architect Seun Oduwole is working on the JK Randle Centre for Yoruba Culture and History. The exhibition and event space will tell the story of the indigenous West African people. And at a rooftop apartment on Moloney Street, the hFactor creative community repurposes underused sites into innovative hubs, and hosts parties, clay-making and stone-carving workshops, film screenings and monthly kerbside pop-ups selling vintage clothing. Meanwhile, the Streetlights Collective puts on jam sessions to discover new musical talent.

But will regeneration happen in the full sense? Lagos has a habit of shaping new corners for the rich rather than improving existing areas for ordinary folk. Eko Atlantic City, an ambitious high-end development, is being built on land reclaimed from the ocean, while upscale Lekki lies on a peninsula, its new constructions gradually stretching – or one could say running – away from the metropolis. But global warming makes it prone to flooding. After the deluge of 2017 a crocodile washed up on the pavement, a reminder that here even the well off are never far from the edge of life. Ironically, those best prepared for climate change are the residents of Makoko, a shanty village of stilt houses and boats known as the Venice of Africa. Its problems – overcrowding, floods, ever-widening wealth gaps – are a microcosm of the planet's problems. And in that sense Lagos is perhaps more forward-facing than we realise. It has done incredibly well to function without imploding, its people always finding ways to adapt, thrive and survive. The city is the past and the future, with the capacity to move in either direction.

This piece is dedicated to all those who died during the #EndSARS movement in October 2020. Those young people, who joined the protests to demand dignity and freedom, are testament to Lagos's enduring spirit. May their energy and defiance live on.

EAGLES, EDGES AND EDIFICES: TOUCHING THE HEAVENS IN TIGRAY, ETHIOPIA

Joey Tyson

For *Suitcase* magazine
February 2020

Feet bare, belly pressed against a slab of rock, I inch my way along the ledge. The grainy surface feels oddly reassuring, given that beyond its edge lurks a sheer 200-m drop. Across the gorge, a row of flat-topped cliffs rise abruptly like a set of colossal teeth; a lone eagle hovers lazily above the void. The next careful steps lead into a small cave, a locked wooden door improbably etched in the cliff side – we have beaten the priest to his church. "He's on his way," explains Zelasie, our guide. By that, he means that the man with the key is currently clambering up a vertical wall of stone, as we had moments earlier.

At the base of the wall we'd stood perplexed as we were told to remove our shoes in respect. A group of men sat idle in its shade. Above, only an ever-expanding tower of sandstone. To the untrained eye, this looked like a dead end. To the waiting scouts on hand to help us climb, it's a sort of rustic ladder, pocked and marked by centuries of the climbing devout. In a moment of *Free Solo*-inspired madness, I'd turned down the rope harness on offer, opting to go it alone – well, not quite alone. As the scouts pointed out the best hand- and footholds, climbing became a vertical game of Twister:

"Left foot here! Right hand there! No, this right, not that one!"

Upwards four and a half metres and one dizzying ledge walk later, a simple padlock remains the last obstacle to Abuna Yemata Guh, the church cut straight into a cliff face. It's one of around 120 in Tigray, Ethiopia. A mountainous expanse of bare, razor-edged peaks jutting from flat plains of arid desert-like scrubland, the country's most northerly region is shrouded in myth and legend, none more captivating than its bizarre rock-hewn churches. Here in the jagged Gheralta massif there are 30 or so. Carved into solid rock, hidden atop mountains and hollowed out of vertiginous cliff sides, they're some of the most obscure and hard-to-reach places of worship on earth. Despite this, the churches are still very much in use, serving the local community as they have done for hundreds of years.

Ethiopia's unique brand of Orthodox Christianity took hold in Tigray in the fourth century, when King Ezana of Axum became the first monarch to embrace it. By local estimations, the churches of Tigray aren't much younger, dating back as far as the fifth century. The history surrounding them is hazy at best with little known about why they are so improbably placed, carved out of the sides of mountains. One theory is to escape destruction: while current-day Ethiopian Christians and Muslims get along peacefully, they didn't always. Back in the Middle Ages, inter-religious tension could easily boil over into the razing of a church.

But these impractical locations weren't solely for practical reasons. At least some of the reasoning, according to Zelasie, was good old-fashioned biblical sadism. Getting there is part of the test, he tells me, one only the truly devout (and a few crazy "ferenjis" – Ethiopians' word for foreigners) pass. As we wait for the priest, and my heart rate drops back to its normal, non-petrified rhythm, Zelasie explains that going to church is a regular part of the weekly routine in Tigray. The local flock will scale its 4.5-m wall, shuffling across its perilous ledge without a second thought. Even new mothers, newborns tightly swaddled on their backs, make the climb to baptise their babies.

Zelasie is something of a regular at Abuna Yemata Guh; he was here a few weeks ago for a special mass in celebration of the church. More than 100 people made the precarious climb to worship, he says. I try to imagine that many people, teetering on boulders, perched on these narrow ledges, gathered in prayer

2,580 m above sea level. The thought alone makes my stomach drop like a faulty lift.

Eventually, a young man arrives on the ledge. He's shrouded in a robe, dove-white – the colour of happiness in Ethiopia – and, despite the ascent, looks calmer than a sloth on Valium. With a small nod of hello, he unlocks the door and beckons us inside. It's dark in the church, the only light coming from a hazy shaft of sun streaming through the entrance. As my eyes adjust, I ask about the young man's age – in his early twenties, surely this is the youngest priest in Ethiopia.

"This is the priest's son, Atsbha," explains Zelasie. A young deacon – a priest in training – he's been entrusted with the church key as the priest himself is running late. Inside, the church is simple, a small cave with carpeted floors and painted murals covering its roof. With no wind, rain or sun exposure, the images on the ceiling have been perfectly preserved. Like a biblical comic book, the stories of Christianity plaster the roof – depictions of the Nine Saints who helped spread the religion through Ethiopia in the fifth century, the 12 Apostles, and Abuna Yemata, the church's founder.

We're alone: a rare treat, I'm told. The young deacon picks up an ancient leather-bound Bible, opening it for us to look at. Beautifully vivid images cover the pages: priests and saints, oval-eyed and depicted in inks of red, yellow, and blue. "When I come here, I lose everything. I feel free. It's not like anywhere else. It is a special place," says Atsbha, leafing through the pages, now jaundiced and greasy with age. I have to agree, even as a non-believer something eerily ethereal hangs heavy in the air. His wide eyes are glassy as he tells of his plan to dedicate his life to the church and the community, just as his father has. We leave Atsbha contemplating his future and begin our trek to another nearby church.

We visit Maryam Korkor, a monastery church devoted to the Virgin Mary. The hike is a punishing two-hour scramble over boulders and through narrow rock passages. Less vertiginous but no less demanding than the trek to the previous church, at points we're surrounded by nothing but rubble and stone, no trace of a route, until Zelasie points out the next "path". In the distance, we see the cliffs of Abuna Yemata Guh – a series of sandstone pinnacles, the tallest pointing skywards like a gargantuan finger.

The church sits atop a mountain plateau surrounded by a serene garden of menorah-shaped giant cacti. When we arrive, sweaty and bedraggled, the resident monk is sitting alone beneath the vaulted arches of the church, cocooned in a brilliant canary-yellow robe, a crucifix clutched in his hands. A large tour group has just left and a quiet, cool peace fills the space. Maryam Korkor is semi-monolithic: a half-building, fixed onto a cave, carved from the mountain. Four tall, stone pillars stand at its centre.

For more than 70 years the monk has called this place home, 400 breath-stealing metres of ascent away from the rest of the world. Even here, other priests and deacons regularly seek out his council. The remote location, 2,400 m above sea level, suggests that this is a place for the devout – the gruelling trek to reach it certainly feels like a test plucked from the Old Testament – but Ethiopia's increasing popularity has led to an influx of travellers. At first, the monk wasn't keen on all the attention, but after the government intervened to make Tigray's churches easier to visit, he's accepted the regular tourist visits. I suspect he'd rather have the peace, and we leave him alone to pray before another group arrives.

My feet feel like boulders as we trudge back down to earth. As the adrenaline wears off, I quickly realise just how shattered I am. But despite my exhausted legs, my mind is completely clear. Looking out over Gheralta's landscape of soaring spires, I wonder if that's the reason these churches were built up here, as close to God as humanly possible.

HOW I TRAVEL AS A BLACK WOMAN

Lola Akinmade Åkerström

For *High Life* magazine
September 2020

I've spent a lifetime decoding them. Those slow crawls of curiosity over my dark skin whenever I find myself exploring a new place. Stares so prolonged that they can unsettle the most intrepid of travellers.

I try to deduce whether they symbolise intrigue, acceptance or rejection. If accompanied by a slight jaw-drop, they're coming from older women and middle-aged men. Teenagers and married men use every reflective surface to covertly observe. Senior citizens in tiny villages stop and freeze. Some stares contort in confusion when I show up at their luxury lodges. Kids point, gawk and giggle.

But the most difficult of all to stomach are the glares that seem to say they wish I didn't exist.

We all experience travel differently, sometimes on a much deeper level than we're even aware of. When I feel the urge to explore and enrich my life by experiencing other cultures, people often question whether there's a more sinister reason driving this need. When I leave my bubble of familiarity to travel and put my life in context as a global citizen, some demand a deeper reason beyond me wanting to gorge on exquisite Sicilian food, trace the steps of Egyptian history or marvel in awe at intricate Uzbek architecture.

Because to travel as a Black woman for leisure or on assignment is to be wordlessly asked to explain my existence in that very space. The deep enrichment travel brings into my life isn't enough. My unwitting task as a traveller who happens to be Black means having constantly to battle the stereotypes of prostitute, impoverished immigrant or low-income worker. In addition to exploration, I also have to rewrite narratives that are continually perpetuated around the world on my behalf.

When I was chased out of a store in Luxembourg and told to look in through their windows instead, a fellow shopper – a stranger

– ran out after me. She chased uphill after me, stopping to pant in exhaustion, her hands on her knees, before proceeding to apologise profusely on behalf of the rude retailer. Maybe that shopkeeper was having a bad day or was simply racist – I will never know – but I always remember that stranger who apologised.

Travelling as a Black woman is a constant emotional minefield of wondering how to not let a singular negative experience derail the gift that travel is endowing me with in that moment.

As a travel writer and photographer, my professional beat is exploring culture through food, tradition and lifestyle. I love sharing the rich stories of the people I meet, their daily lives, the customs they fiercely protect – and what makes them burn with unbridled passion. Travelling with an open mind is easier said than done because it forces us to ask questions of other cultures and of ourselves. And it begins the uncomfortable work of chipping away at our own preconceived notions about people, places and practices.

For me, travel is about being a sponge. I soak up other cultures with respect, but I also squeeze some of myself and my culture out in return to foster understanding, break down bias and break through prejudices. It's about doing my own part to fight stereotypes by seeing people for who they are as individuals, and not waving general brushstrokes over an entire group.

And it is exhausting work.

After a long, hot day exploring Samarkand, my travelling companions turned to me, themselves shattered. "How do you do it and not get tired?" they asked me. We were halfway through our trip traversing parts of Uzbekistan and I was being relentlessly asked for dozens upon dozens of selfies with locals. Many of them were fascinated by my presence. Most of them had never seen a Black African woman in person before.

"If I end up being the only Black person they meet in their lifetime, I want that interaction to positively counteract the negative narratives media constantly spread about us," I replied.

As I kept travelling with an open mind over the years, I noticed my heart expanding in parallel. I know when to extend grace based on the type of stares I decode. I also know when to self-preserve and when to receive appreciation without suspicion. I remember standing in a packed yet eerily silent subway car in Stockholm. The subway is a space where everyone stays invisible until they get off to meet their loved ones. In a place where compliments and public acknowledgment aren't doled out with ease, an old woman yelled across that quiet carriage to tell me I was beautiful.

The privilege of travel has filled me with an undeniable resolve and passion to keep exploring and learning about the world around me. Above all, it keeps me truly listening to people and their cultures, to what they believe and why they live the way they do.

The very act of travelling as a Black woman forces strangers to see me, deal with me and learn about me even when they aren't ready to. And, in my own way, I begin to chip slowly away at their biases, distrust and discomfort, one encounter at a time.

EARTH'S
LAST GREAT
WILDERNESS

Stanley Stewart

For *Condé Nast Traveller*
April 2020

Apparently it's a common feeling, this lingering obsession. Looking back now on my time at the end of the world, I am haunted by Antarctica. It feels unreal, dreamlike – those ice lakes scattered with star points of light, the immense snow cliffs with their blue shadows, the gossamer sheen of silver across the ridges of the frozen ocean, the white abstract shapes. Nothing prepares for this place. It is a continent of superlatives – the coldest, driest, highest, windiest space on the planet. But its beauty is what will break your heart.

We had flown south from Cape Town, five and a half hours across the Southern Ocean, unaware of how intoxicating Antarctica would be. There was cloud cover for much of the way, but after three hours the sky cleared and I looked down on icebergs afloat on a sea of intense blue. We were at 35,000 ft, and I suddenly realised the icebergs, calved from the vast continent that lay in wait, were the size of counties.

We landed on a frozen runaway. Having kitted up in the plane – at –10°C, it was a modest four-layer day – we stepped out into that dry, rasping air, into that light so wonderful and so tangible I felt I could gather it up in my hands. Bar some tents and Nissen huts that housed the airstrip's support, it was a vast, empty world. Away to our right, the sculptural sweep of snow and ice was interrupted by sharp-toothed mountains like black cut-outs against a turquoise sky. They gave this runway its name: Wolf's Fang. I was told they were high mountains, but in this fathomless expanse their scale was impossible to judge. Were they huge peaks or mere ridges that one could scamper up in an hour or so? In Antarctica there were no points of reference.

No one owns this continent. There is no passport control when you arrive, no immigration regulations, no border post. In a gentlemanly fashion, countries recognise one another's territorial claims – there are seven in all – in spite of the fact that they are often overlapping and have no legal status. Antarctica is the only place on earth where you are not in any political entity, where you are officially nowhere.

The history is fairly tenuous. For millennia Antarctica remained undiscovered, though people seemed to sense it was there long before anyone had seen it; even ancient Greek scholars spoke of a mysterious southern continent. Some enthusiasts were convinced it would be a fair land of happy people and fertile fields, an idea fortunately abandoned by the time it was first sighted, from the crow's nest of a flagship, just 200 years ago in January 1820.

Since then it has largely been the story of explorers and madmen, chaps with frozen beards and thousand-yard stares. In the empty spaces of Antarctica, they gather around like ghosts. A little more than a century ago, this was still the great unknown, the final blank on the map. As such, it drew men heartbroken at having missed out on dengue fever in the sodden jungles of Borneo or spear wounds in the scramble for Africa. Ernest Shackleton, possibly the most prominent of Antarctic explorers, said it was the last great journey left to man. And of course for some, it would be their last. When Apsley Cherry-Garrard, one of the survivors of Robert Falcon Scott's ill-fated Terra Nova expedition, published his memoir in 1922, the title came easily. He called it *The Worst Journey in the World*.

But Antarctica is never just a journey. It's in the nature of this remarkable place that traversing it is always about something more than the challenges of its geography. Shackleton admitted the continent had become a metaphor for him and for others. "We all have our own White South," he said, alluding to the idea of a quest for meaning and significance. All these adventurers would be obsessed by their time here in the white south for the rest of their lives. It was where they had felt most vividly alive. Years later, sitting in the window of his library, reading his old notebooks as an English afternoon faded across his lawns, Cherry-Garrard wrote a note in the margins, "Can we ever forget those days?"

I should really have been hunkered down inside several sleeping bags, polar blizzards battering the tent, while the dogs howled outside and my hot-water bottle turned to ice. But I confess I wasn't. The Antarctic tour operator White Desert, founded by a couple of modern-day polar travellers, has created itineraries that take the hardship out of discovery. Its base, Whichaway Camp, in the remote spaces of Queen Maud Land in the east, must count as one of the most exclusive stays in the world. The logistics that support it would test a space mission.

The camp consists of seven insulated circular pods, tethered to the ground in case of sudden storms and set apart from one another across one of the few swathes of exposed rock. It looked like the set for a sci-fi film – a human colony stranded on an alien planet. There are six larger domes, three of which make for a spacious communal area with fur throws and a library of books. Cherry-Garrard would have snorted with disgust at such indulgence.

Crucially, as much thought has gone into environmental impact at Whichaway as comfort. Antarctica is ground zero for climate change. It's home to 90 per cent of the world's ice, yet temperatures are rising faster here than almost anywhere else – a rise of 10°F since the 1950s. Should these trends continue, the effect on global sea levels will be catastrophic.

The continent's vulnerability demands respect from those who operate here. White Desert offsets its flights and activities with accredited carbon-neutral schemes. It has pioneered a solar-power system for heat and water, and this year expects to eliminate single-use plastics from its supply chain. All waste is shipped out to be recycled or disposed of responsibly in South Africa. Finally, when the camp's lifespan reaches a natural end, it will be removed without a trace.

Whichaway offers a unique experience. The conventional way to reach the southern continent is on a polar cruise, going ashore via Zodiac boats in regimented excursions to see penguins, seals and other sea life. More than 50,000 people a year visit Antarctica this way. But only about 160 stay at the camp each season, bedding down on the landmass itself. In a small group of five, we took trips on foot, in the camp's six-by-six truck, and in White Desert's Basler BT-67 propeller planes, which acted as our flying taxis to more distant parts. It felt like a rare privilege.

In those summer months, it was never dark. Antarctica was luminous with 24-hour daylight, a neutral canvas painted with rays as the sun gravitated round the sky: the pale milky blue; the rose-tainted mornings; the crisp white of midday; an afternoon blush like yellowed grass; an evening of pearly, smoky greys; the heather-coloured night.

Whichaway sits on the edge of an ice lake, its surface rippled into patterns like frozen winds. One morning we set off across it, our crampons crunching on the surface, towards the cliffs on the far shore. The lake, the cliffs and the frosted fields beyond were a study in minimalist simplicity, a paradise of clean lines, austere, vast, unfussy. But there were details, too: the complex web of cracks and veins in the solid water; the cryoconite holes, with their exquisite lacework of crystals and air bubbles, created by dust or rock pieces trapped in the ice. A section of the cliff broke away on the far side of the lake, and fell with a sound like thunder, shattering the delicate silence.

We climbed over a steep shoulder of snow to a sloping expanse rising to the skyline. Roped together, leaning into the slope, we felt tiny against the magnitude of this place. On the ridge line, we left our crampons in the lee of some rocks and clambered up a nunatak, a stony peak protruding from the glacier. From the summit, we looked out across that bright, silent stillness. Stretches of snow and ice tipped away into fathomless distances without the interruption of a single alien feature, bar our own trail of footprints below. This must be what infinity looks like, I thought.

No one lives on Antarctica; even the hardy souls who overwinter in scientific research stations are really only visitors. But it is not just human inhabitants that are missing. Life of any kind is scarce – and what does exist can be a little strange. No trees or shrubs grow here; flora is limited to lichen, moss and algae.

The largest land animal that permanently occupies Antarctica is the wingless midge, which grows to just half an inch. The chief birds include snow petrels and skuas. The snow petrels – white calligraphic figures on blue skies – feed mainly on fish, while the large, gull-like skuas feed on the chicks of petrels and other birds; their nests are surrounded by graveyards of bleached bones. Skuas lay two eggs so that one of the chicks, in this land of sparse resources, can be fed to the other.

In startling contrast to the land, the surrounding seas are teeming with life, supported by shrimp-like krill, the basis of the marine food chain here, which has, at an estimated 500 million tonnes, the largest biomass of any animal species on the planet. Numerous whales come to the Southern Ocean to feed, including blue whales, the earth's largest creature. There are also southern elephant seals, Antarctic fur seals and leopard seals, among others. Finally, and most famously, there are the penguins, who feed at sea but breed on land or ice.

Everyone seems to have watched the saga of the heroic male emperor penguin nursing a single egg through the gales of winter while the females depart in search of food.

Near Neumayer III research station we visited a penguin rookery, a few miles inland away from the threat of carnivorous leopard seals. As we approached, the gathered birds sounded like a chicken coop. A chorus of squawking and squeaking rose from the cold assembly. In a society where everyone has turned up in the same tuxedo, voices are important; individuals locate one another by vocalisation.

Mid-winter, in a howling gale, the penguins are all fearless grit and cold flippers. But in this season, mid-summer, the colony felt pleasantly aimless, even idle. They were just hanging out, as if at a garden party, nattily dressed, shuffling their feet, making small talk, waiting for the drinks tray to come around again. Occasionally one flops down for ice surfing, paddling on its belly like a torpedo-shaped toboggan, before slowly getting to its feet again. The youngsters, fluffy, impossibly cute, have the gleeful look of children allowed to stay up past their bedtime for a grown-up gathering.

David Attenborough has called the life of the emperor penguin one of nature's greatest acts of survival, as well as one of its most romantic love stories. Emperor society is considerate and kindly; it is primarily about happy families. Down on the coast, male elephant seals are tearing each others' throats out before mating with every female they can lay their flippers on. But male emperors are sensitive fellows, loyal to their wives, eager to share childcare. They coo affectionately at their spouses, who coo back. Then both coo at their single child. From time to time, one of the parents starts to gag, then leans over and vomits fish into the little one's waiting mouth. Even this is managed with decorum.

Another day, we went to the seaside. The Southern Ocean was frozen solid. For 60 miles or more a rumpled apron of sea stretched outward from the shore to the open water. It is not a flat ice sheet but a tumultuous upheaval of colossal, rock-solid waves, most taller than a man. Sunlight cascaded over their shoulders like liquid silver. In the troughs between them lay shadows of watery blue.

Standing there, on the edge of the ocean, I felt in awe of this place, of its scale, its splendour, its beauty. And with that awe, my own life, with all its anxieties and concerns, its minor triumphs and rather less minor failures, its pain and its hurts, shrank away. It was a wonderful feeling, the amazement and the accompanying loss of self, as profound as meditation. It was liberating. In that sparkling moment, in the crystal air of Antarctica, I thought, there can be no better journey, no better destination than this exhilarating feeling of liberation. Even when it means going to the end of the earth to find it.

A LONGING
TO MOVE

Michelle Jana Chan

For *Vanity Fair*
November 2020

Think back to last year. At any given moment, there were about a million people up in the air on a plane. Many more would have been on the move at ground level, in cars, buses, boats and trains, or on foot, whether commuters, refugees, business travellers or holidaymakers. It was a time of the greatest recorded movement of humankind.

But that was last year, and the years before last year.

This is this year.

I'm in the Serengeti in northern Tanzania. Around me are tens of thousands of wildebeest, an animal with surely one of the best names. Though it looks less savage than it sounds. As individuals, they are not markedly impressive with their elongated jaws, scraggly beards and modest horns. But collectively they cut a striking herd. En masse, as they are now, kicking up the dust around me, they become wild, beast-like; a stampede of speed that feels dynamic, dangerous. One individual accelerates suddenly, another follows. Some mosey, meander. But most move at a pace, head down, doggedly focused. This cyclical migration of two million wildebeest – circling from Tanzania up to Kenya's Masai Mara, in search of greener pastures, then back south, always pursuing the rains – is one of the world's greatest continuous journeys.

It turns out that while many of us are standing still, many others are still moving.

I love the wide open spaces of the Rift Valley, its dearth of landmarks, the feeling you can become easily lost. I also love it for its cradling of the history of humankind, the interring of some of the oldest known specimens of hominins. Our early ancestors perhaps also felt the sense of freedom that this land gives me, when they hauled themselves up from all fours, stood straight, and with extra height stared out at the horizon.

The allure of the Serengeti is profound, yet some travellers have long written off this place, particularly at certain times of year when tourists were coming in droves to watch the megaherds of wildebeest confront the fast-flowing Mara River, facing off crocodiles, lions and other predators. The crossings make for serious wildlife action – and opportunities for powerful photography. But swing the camera around and hundreds of safari vehicles can be seen jostling on the banks, the guides under pressure to secure the best vantage.

But that was last year, and the years before last year.

This is this year. It is deserted now.

My first day, mine was the only vehicle waiting on the banks of the Mara. My guide Hamza Visram and I had staked out beneath the shadow of an acacia tree, a few hundred metres away from the river, on an incline, so we had height to study the direction the herds were moving in. The ritual of waiting for a crossing is like war. Nothing much happens, until it does.

From a distance, we sat patiently, studying through binoculars the wildebeest swirling below, tentatively approaching the water, then billowing back. They are perpetually hesitant. Even their lowing sounds of two minds, hemming and hawing: yeah, no, yeah, no, yeah, no. To or fro. To or fro. Indecisive to a point. There might be an unprompted sprint, before they stop abruptly, inexplicably, before circling and retreating. It feels impossible to get into the head of a wildebeest. But perhaps the animal's reluctance is not so odd, given crossing the Mara is a matter of life or death. Then I tilt my head, as I hear the noise escalating. At first, the sound is like the strings section of an orchestra warming up, but that has now morphed, accompanied by snorting and grunting and honking. So much so that the churn of the Mara's rushing water has been drowned out. Something's happening. We fire up the car engine and accelerate down, as the scene becomes frantic. The animals are funnelling down the steep banks. Some are already in the water. I watch them leap, witness the splash. One after another. I can smell pungent wet hide, like wet dog.

This section of the river is deep and they swim awkwardly, carried by the current, making an S-shaped route to reach the other side. In the commotion, hippos rise up, bellowing, agitated. If too threatened, they have been known to snap a wildebeest in half and eat the grass contents of its stomach. All around, crocodiles cruise sentinel, forming a wake with their speed, even in this white water. Amid the pandemonium, on a sandbank, two Egyptian geese stand rooted to the ground, seemingly in shock.

On the opposite side, the wildebeest swarm on to the muddy shallows, too many arriving, too few able to clamber up the sheer edges. In spite of colossal effort, some tumble backwards as they attempt to ascend, their bodies smashing upon the previous, breaking their backs, done for.

Time to time, I become invested in one particular animal. Perhaps it is slightly smaller or older, more vulnerable. I zone in on one now, gunning for its survival. Somehow it makes it across, past the expectant crocodiles, but when it reaches the shallows, I worry it will be crushed in the fray. It jostles, re-entering the river, washed downstream until it lands at an easier exit point. It's got lucky. I privately cheer, as it joins its brethren, their wet backs shining with success.

And then strangely – you couldn't make it up – one swims back towards me. It's unclear why. Perhaps a mother separated from its young? But that wouldn't explain why large breakaway groups of several dozen also make the muddled journey back. Risking their lives again. And then once more, as they realise their error. As if one crossing wasn't hard enough, they do it three times. Statistically, that's hard to survive.

On my side, the outpouring of wildebeest suddenly stops in their tracks. Perhaps they're spooked. Or a maverick breaks with the herd mentality and halts. Arrested, the front row stares down at the rough water below, as if summoning courage. Hours pass. This kind of wildlife viewing is about time, which becomes even more distilled when alone; we're still the only ones here. We've almost lost the light when a brave individual bolts, and the rest copy. Thousands make the leap, mostly victoriously, but not always.

I watch a robust adult wildebeest carried downstream, probably injured; there seems to be resignation in its eyes. Then, more predictably, a baby is taken, releasing a yelp as it's pulled under by a crocodile. Simultaneously I see another snapped up further downstream. I think about these juveniles being born earlier in the year in the southern Serengeti, learning to walk miraculously within minutes of their births, with jackals and hyenas hounding them. After all that, this.

We all know travel has its risks.

The number of wildebeest carcasses is piling up along the river, in the nooks of rocks, heaps of dead bodies, their angular legs sticking up in the air. Some float past like driftwood; there is one with a Rüppell's griffon vulture riding on its bloated belly, pecking through the thick hide. Flanking the river, hundreds of birds congregate, the hooded, lappet-faced and white-backed vultures, all in a flap to pick up the scraps.

Although many come to the Serengeti for the drama of the Mara crossings, I still prefer the wide open plains. The next day I'm up before dawn, Venus still bright in the sky. We drive east, the low sun straight in our eyes, squinting in the dust and the cold wind.

Ahead, in the distance, there are bands of wildebeest inching along the horizon; nearer, sometimes single file as columns, or messy sporadic herds with their lolloping rise-and-fall motion. Up close, their posture is low-slung, head down, their gaze inscrutable; the collective noun is rightly an implausibility of wildebeest. Around, dust devils swirl, before blowing themselves out.

There's nowhere else I'd rather be than here. But I had heard, distractingly, that Ngorongoro Crater was devoid of tourists, too; visiting now was like a throwback to the 1960s, when few knew about this extraordinary site: one of the world's largest intact caldera. Because of the altitude and limited passes over the rim, many of the animals born here, stay here. It's like the game is on tap.

Over the past few decades, as travellers learned about this place, they came in increasing numbers to see the ring-fenced 30,000-odd hectares. "In recent years there were probably twice as many vehicles than there should have been," Hamza says. "Sometimes there were twenty cars on a lion sighting."

But that was last year, and the years before last year.

This is this year.

Ours is the only vehicle in the crater. Looking across the expanse of greens, yellows and beiges, soft undulations, layers of haze, a shrunken lake shimmering, the land wobbles in the heat. Shadow of clouds pattern the crater floor. The solitude is acute. Pausing by zebra, I notice I can hear them chewing, their teeth grinding. From a distance, there is the clunk of horn on horn as two wildebeest rut. There's the buzz of a bee, as I separately smack a tsetse. There's something sweet-smelling in the air, wild mint or basil.

We drive through a copse of fever trees, where great white pelicans, yellow-billed storks and sacred ibis are congregating in marshland. A handsome bat-eared fox peeps out of a burrow, darts back in, emerges again. Alongside the vehicle, there is a flash of the white wings of the northern anteater-chat, flying with effort into wind. Pairs of grey crowned cranes stand tall among the swaying grasses, seemingly uncomfortable with their own beauty. I spy a green pigeon, fluffed up in the crook of a ficus tree.

On the dusty road, because of the few cars, tracking has become much easier; there are no tyre tracks except our own. We pull over to inspect: the four-toed webbed prints of hippo, beside signature porcupine with their telltale striation patterns in the sand, then the clawed pug marks of hyena.

The safari experience has changed in other ways, too. When we come upon three lionesses, they tear off. "They're more skittish than they used to be," Hamza says. "They've become unfamiliar with tourists." We find a family of hippo out of the water in the late morning, still grazing; usually, they'd be back in their pools. "Without disturbances, they feel safer," Hamza says. "Life is simple now for them, nobody is coming."

We spot three rhino; it turns out it's easier to see rhino than another safari vehicle.

That afternoon, I take a hike with Peter Saruni, a local Masai. Usually he conducts cultural tours around his village of Nainokanoka but all that is on hold because of the coronavirus. Together we climb Olmoti crater, before trekking down to the falls of the Munge river.

The armed ranger who walks with us, Edna Kitatung'wa, hasn't joined a hike like this since March when the virus halted nearly all travel to the region, but she remains sanguine. "I hope the tourists come back next month," she says. It felt like I was watching a film, knowing something the protagonists don't.

Before we part, I watch a lesser striped swallow in a tree, its distinctive rounded head, its pert beak, its forked tail flitting to stay balanced on a twig. These petite birds are big travellers, even mightier migrants than the wildebeest, flying distances from Sierra Leone to South Africa. So fragile, yet undeterred. Listening to their instinct. Wanting to fly. Unable not to.

CURRENT AFFAIRS

Rae Boocock

For *Suitcase* magazine
January 2020

I'd walked more than 160 km for this meal. With a twinging ankle, I'd scuttled sideways, crablike, along the paths that fall from the Western Heights into Dover. Sunburnt and spent, I flounder into a chippy for no reason other than that its name, Wheeler's, reminds me of that oyster place in Whitstable. Turns out this one is a Marco Pierre White outfit, but the waiting area has good air con and it's 30 degrees outside.

I carry my takeaway to watch the liners from the harbour, slightly irked to have been handed a box decorated with faux newspaper print. Are those sachets of ketchup? Full-size cutlery? I lift the lid to a thimble of tartare sauce and a lemon wedge. Inside crisp batter, the cod flakes neatly; the chips are stiff. Yet what I really want is to unpick them from a mass sodden with vinegar. A few salty shards of batter. A dip of gravy. I want to give up on a futile little fork and eat with my fingers as grease soaks through the paper to my knees. I want a proper chippy tea, and restaurants just aren't up to it.

My walk had started four days earlier in Brighton, though it had been tiptoeing around my mind for a decade before that. As part of a Thatcherism module at university, I'd read *Coasting*, Jonathan Raban's account of sailing around Britain, a country he finds divided by class, an insular nation clinging to a fairy tale of our green and pleasant land. He was writing in 1982, but it's hard not to draw comparisons to the world of today, with record levels of unemployment, economic recession, a Tory government, a tug-of-power with the EU and headlines etched with the language of war – albeit one now waged against a virus, not Argentinians.

I'm taken by Raban's idea that Britain's identity can be sought at its perimeter. The tidal pull has been particularly strong in my life – I grew up on the north-west coast and, after a stint in the capital, washed up in Brighton. But in the grand scheme of things, no Brit is more than 120 km from the sea. I want to gaze into our fourth, watery wall and see what of us is reflected back.

Unlike Raban, I possess not the slightest inclination to play captain. Instead, I would follow the England Coast Path, a 4,500-km sea-hugging route – the longest of its kind in the world – that will fill in the gaps left between existing trails by the time it's launched in 2021, the preordained "Year of the English Coast". An internet search tells me that it would take the best part of four months to walk the lot, so I settle on two manageable sections: from Brighton to Dover – home now – and Fleetwood to Liverpool – home then.

Starting a walking trip from your flat is rather unmomentous. I smother my two cats with kisses and take the bins out as I leave; nip back with post from the corridor. Heading to the pier, I pass a group on The Level who, at 7 a.m., have lit a fire and several zoots. On London Road, I glance down a ginnel at the moment a guy crouches for a shit. So far, so Brighton.

It's only after I'm through the marina, the white splinter of the Undercliff piercing the horizon, that I feel like I'm doing something greater than trekking to the big Asda. Over the next few days, I trace a coastline crumbling under the weight of its own history. I pass Peacehaven's prime meridian, cross the brackish Cuckmere Haven and scramble up the whale's maw of the Seven Sisters. There are nine climbs on this rippling stretch between Seaford and Eastbourne – a point I imagine more people would make a fuss about if they walked it with a heavy rucksack.

Caught between day trippers, I walk in tandem with two men whose conversation ricochets through the wavesong. "We need to think of a better word for the working class than 'gammons'." "Yup." "Meritocracy." "Yah." I pass a woman dressed head-to-toe in white who has pitched up with a guitar, a violin player and a tripod, and is reciting the kirtan *Ong Namo*. "I'm coming home. I'm coming home," she chants. I feel quite far from home.

The ice-cream-scooped edges of the south coast become amphitheatres of the places from where I come and go. One morning, inhaling a fried-egg sandwich between boats moored around Pevensey Bay – Bad Buoys, The Reel Thing, Fat Git – I see Beachy Head back west. Out front is Dungeness, the post-apocalyptic fantasy land where I'd wander among the sun-bleached ribcages of much older vessels the following afternoon.

I have no map. I am guided by the topography of the coast. In the areas the sea slips from view, tidal energy permeates clapboard cottages, rock shops strung with inflatables and herds of static caravans. At the unbridged River Rother, it takes three hours to divert inland through Rye, a saccharine town which sat on the coast before its harbour silted up. It's a brief interlude on a busy road and, over thundering cars, my mind replays the coastal orchestra: the cymbal crash of waves, rattling grasses on the strings, my boots on percussion, crunching through scrub. Black-headed gulls take the melody.

That night I'm staying in Camber and, as I cross fields back towards the sea, the light has gone almost completely and Google Maps is glitching. I call my mum who, through the power of a shared WhatsApp location and motivational hyping, successfully escorts me to bed. I wonder at what age I'll grow out of this.

England's vulnerable underbelly is a testament to nature's power to give and take. Such is the might of Poseidon, the Olympian god of the ocean, flood and drought. According to Environment Agency data, rising sea levels mean that vast stretches of the route I walk today will be underwater within a century. I see two sea walls under construction and lose count of the signs reading "Erosion. Route diversion." I pass Belle Tout, a lighthouse hauled 17 m backwards from the Seven Sisters' receding edge. The Winchelsea through which I travel is, in fact, New Winchelsea; the original town was consumed by storms in the thirteenth century. "Are you looking for the coastal path, darling?" a woman asks me in Hastings' gill woodland, her dog nosing the crisp packet in my pocket. "Just duck under the landslide sign, we all do."

I'm grateful for this lady. Between Ecclesbourne Glen and the Firehills, I navigate a twisted rock face matted with mosses, ferns and overhanging trees. For a couple of hours, the only souls I see are two wild Exmoor ponies grazing among the heather. Yet it's in the footsteps of man that I discover a coast carved by defence against more mortal enemies. In Fairlight, between cottages named Ozone and Calais View, a plane propeller plays garden centrepiece alongside a rain-streaked information card about the Battle of Britain. I pick up the Saxon Shore Way, along which Romans built defensive forts in 270 BCE, stop at squat Martello Towers and schlep around Lydd Firing Range to the sound mirrors at Romney Marsh.

The next day on Hythe Beach, I breakfast on deliciously pungent kippers as silhouettes cast out into a creased-silk sea, before tracing the Royal Military Canal. En route, I think about a Second World War-era poster I'd spied in Hastings town centre. Below a rendering of a shepherd on the South Downs shoreline it read: "Your Britain. Fight for it now." This coast is to die for.

After a swim by Sandgate's pastel huts, I cherry-pick the artwork in Folkestone's open-air exhibition: Tracey Emin, Yoko Ono and, under the Harbour Arm, one of Antony Gormley's Another Time figures eyeballing France. By the time I reach Dover, the continent is about 30 km off – a distance less than I'd walked most days. My mobile service provider switches to SFR. The day I arrive, 16 refugees have crossed from Calais to Kingsdown and MPs are rowing over the Internal Market Bill. On my newsfeed, I see charades of patriotism; Britain standing defiantly against European neighbours and anyone who might seek safety on our shores. In real life, Vera Lynn's White Cliffs look grimy. I squint at France on the horizon.

In Fleetwood, it's easier to make out the Lake District across Morecambe Bay. I'd travelled up to my parents' the night before, greeted by three excitable dogs and mum's pièce de résistance: lasagne and crumble. "Noel and Doreen came around with three full bags of apples," she said, putting on her burdened voice, though I could tell she was delighted. It tasted like home.

In *Notes from a Small Island*, Bill Bryson calls the view from Fleetwood Esplanade "one of the most beautiful in the world". He's not wrong. When I arrive just after sunrise, the tide is out and the yawning bay is rippled with the mauve reflections of morning. It's somehow softer here. The local herring gull gossips quietly, the promenade is curvaceous, shingle has become sand. A down-to-earth warmth radiates from the people too. Against the grumble of the A587 and the click-thud screech of trams, the soundtrack of my northern leg is "Morrrnin". "Yorite luv?" "T'Liverpool yer walkin'? Shit."

I feel a bit different here, too. In the south, beyond Brighton, I was discovering my adopted home. Here, the coast is awash with memories. That time we got caught by the tide on Cleveleys Beach and when the Riverdance ferry ran aground, spilling its cargo of McVitie's digestives; school trips to The Beatles museum at Liverpool's Albert Dock; orthodontist appointments on St Annes' seafront; sticking our heads out of the sunroof as dad drove through Blackpool illuminations.

But in the harsh light of 2020, the north-west has a different sheen. By day, the illuminations lose their magic. Approaching the North Pier, I pass more hotel fronts with missing letters than complete signs. Ponies pull Cinderella-style carriages past shops emblazoned with "Cut-price rock!" "We sell cigarettes!" "Gypsy Lavinia! This lady has predicted for GMTV!" A tannoy from Pat's 10p Prize Bingo fizzles: "Eyes down. Yellow. Key of the door, 21. Red. Big Ben, number 10. Winner winner chicken dinner." A woman dressed as Ariel warbles Disney songs while a middle-aged Sebastian tap-dances alongside, an old *Britain's Got Talent* number pinned beside an open suitcase. I try (and fail) not to cast my mind back to the buskers at Seaford.

Though it bears all the totems of a seaside holiday, the Fylde Peninsula isn't all fun and games. As if competing, its statistics are cut by phrases such as "Britain's unhealthiest community", "highest antidepressant usage" and "most-deprived area". Once the UK's third-largest port, Fleetwood was devastated by the Icelandic cod wars of the 1970s and fishing quotas set by the EEC (later the EU) in 1983. Here, Leavers sold Brexit as an opportunity to rewrite these unfavourable rules, and it's no surprise they won. I voted Remain, but on referendum day, while I felt sad about the result, I felt sadder still that my social media was littered with one-liners about the xenophobic, imbecile north where I'd grown up. This was the chasm between north and south, between the metropole and drowning coastal towns.

Where the south seems scarred by climate change and conflicts past, in the north, the tributes I see have a more intimate, modern flavour. In Fleetwood, a statue entitled "Welcome Home" depicts a mother and children gazing expectantly to sea for their father. Fishermen are fabled here. Another sculpture reads: "Their courage and comradeship under hardship is living legend." Alongside it are names of boats and locations. Twelve lost. Three lost. All hands. Just down the coast, four Angel of the North-style figures pay homage to Lancashire's emergency services. I walk across the dunes of St Annes, yellow as butter, melting into Lytham. A fighter jet scratches into Warton airfield, an outpost of BAE Systems, the UK's largest defence company and one of Lancashire's biggest employers. Both my parents worked there.

That evening I tuck into fish and chips the northern way, my way: haddock with gravy, curry sauce and a cuppa. When I said that restaurants aren't up to serving fish and chips, what I meant is that I don't like restaurants' fish and chips. I'm not sure I'm going to find a collective identity on our coast, but from the places I've been, it seems that a lot of us are hell-bent on defending things – whether battling the elements, foreign power or being a pedant about your chippy tea. You know the way you like yours. Maybe that's what Britishness is. The seafront is our home front is our frontline. It's no wonder that Second World War ministers bent over backwards to make sure fish and chips were never rationed.

The next morning, this epiphany has me feeling down as I set off from Southport. Behind me, Blackpool's Pepsi Max roller coaster has become a man-made crest among the Lakeland peaks. I pull my feet over Formby's shifting dunes knitted together by marram grass and reclaimed Christmas trees. On the shore, shipwrecks and Neolithic footprints peer from sandy graves.

At Crosby, for the second time in my journey, my horizon is punctuated by one of Antony Gormley's iron men. The tide comes in quickly, waves pushing the ring of scum up his motionless body.

From the back of his knees, it rises over his wrists, buttocks, waist, shoulders, until the tip of his head, crowning between ripples, is the only sign that anything had ever been there at all. It reminds me of a Stevie Smith poem I read in school:

> Nobody heard him, the dead man,
> But still he lay moaning:
> I was much further out than you thought
> And not waving but drowning.

I feel suffocated. Is "Brits love defending things" the thing that's really jumped out at me from this beautiful walk? Sure, you can put a triumphant spin on it, but this beleaguered independence feels rather lonely.

In the Port of Liverpool, Everton has proposed to build a football ground by 2024, but today the buildings on its outskirts remind me of aged men. Weeds sprout through the nostrils of their air vents; like neglected skin, their paintwork is blistered and peeling. I pass a rubbish tip topped by an upturned Henry hoover smiling mawkishly; and electrical boxes tagged by Sine Missone, the Scouse Banksy. "There never was a good war or bad peace".

Past the Royal Liver Building, Pier Head and Albert Dock are from another world. The sharp angles of the Museum of Liverpool give way to the Tate and statues of the city's "Fab Four". And yet it's here, serendipitously, that I see a cluster of tucked-away war memorials, each dedicated to servicepeople from outside Britain: the Netherlands, Belgium Poland, Norway, China. "For those who gave their lives for this country, thank you."

The coast of Great Britain, including the islands, stretches more than 30,000 km. For one week, in one strange year, I had walked less than one per cent of that distance. In that snapshot of time and place, between chalk cliffs and faded seaside towns, I had passed through communities that are as diverse as the lands they inhabit and yet united by a determination to defend.

There are stats floating around that those living near the shore are happiest. But I'm not convinced by this myth of a coastal population high off sea air. On Rossall Beach a sign reads: "Plants that grow on shingle or sand are specially adapted to the harsh environment." And I think this rings more true of the people with whom I cross paths on the coast than any study can prove.

Setting off, I had been naive to think of the sea as a fourth wall. It's a port; a reminder that there are horizons beyond ourselves, at home and away. No man is an island. If Britain's fringe harbours our spirit, it's here I feel buoyant about a future in which differences needn't mean we drift apart. So long as I have gravy with my chips.

INTO THE UNKNOWN

Sophy Roberts

For *The Financial Times*
March 2020

When I open the pages of my notepad to write this story, I can smell the desert: that dry, scorched aroma belonging to a place elsewhere – a landscape so far off it feels like a kind of promised land. It was January when I went to Chad's remote Ennedi Massif – a 40,000-sq-km plateau about the size of Switzerland, which in 2016 was recognised as a UNESCO World Heritage Site and has more recently been the focus for significant conservation work through the NGO African Parks. Months later, in lockdown in rural England, the grains of sand clinging to the notebook's pages seem to me as fantastical as tiny shavings of stars, each bleached particle a stowaway from another time.

But these fragmented memories of place, and the news of small wildlife successes in the middle of a pandemic, shouldn't sugar-coat the complexities that make up this region's extraordinary story. Ennedi is part of the predominantly Muslim north-east of this former French colony. Chad is a landlocked country, one side of it Saharan, the other scrubby, semi-arid Sahel, with barely any infrastructure. After independence in 1960, political chaos led to violent tensions and by the mid-1960s Chad had tumbled into one of Africa's longest-running civil wars. In 1990, the military commander Idriss Déby entered the capital N'Djamena unopposed. Thirty years on, he's still in power.

These days, there are some reasonable hotels (many of them busy with the Chinese workforce building Africa's mines and roads) and a French pâtisserie, L'Amandine, selling dainty macarons. Chad is more secure than its immediate neighbours – Libya to the north, Sudan to the east, the Central African Republic to the south, Cameroon and Nigeria to the south-west, and Niger to the west – but that's no great boast: Chad's proximity to these troubled nations doesn't put it at the top of any tourist bucket list because it also has security risks of its own.

The UK foreign office has turned Chad into a swathe of red (advising against all travel) and yellow (advising against all but essential travel). Logistics are challenging, even for Africa, with unreliable sheduled domestic flights. There are private charters to Fada, which is the historical capital of the Ennedi region. Alternatively, you travel here by road from N'Djamena, which involves a tough two-day drive.

But what looks bad on Google isn't always the whole story. In 2015, I visited Chad for the first time to report on a story about elephant conservation. On my last night in N'Djamena, I got talking with an Italian called Rocco Ravà at the hotel bar; he was running a specialist desert tour company founded by his parents, Piero Ravà and Marina Clessi. Their expertise was the central Sahara, including the Ennedi Plateau and the Tibesti Mountains in the country's north.

Piero, an experienced alpinist, had first come to Africa to work as a doctor in Kenya in the early 1970s. He fell in love with the desert on the overland journey back home to Milan in 1975, and returned two years later with his young family and two four-wheel drives to lead tourist expeditions – first in Algeria, then Niger, Mali and Chad, shifting their geography as Saharan politics ebbed and flowed. "The dunes were my playground, where there was only one rule," says Ravà of his childhood in the Saharan sands. "I wasn't allowed to break up the crests until the tourists had been, so their photographs looked pristine."

By the age of 25, Ravà was helping his father provide expedition logistics for the Frenchman Théodore Monod, one of the most significant Sahara researchers of the twentieth century. But it was by no means easy. In 1998, Ravà was leading a group of trekkers on Emi Koussi volcano in Tibesti when his party was ambushed by six armed rebels. Two of the foreigners were taken hostage. Ravà, conversing in French, negotiated with the kidnappers; he told them to take him, not his clients, which they agreed to. All night the rebels marched him over the volcano. On the third night, when one of them asked why he didn't complain, he answered them in Chadian Arabic, with a few words of the local Toubou language. "They realised then that I wasn't a classic white man," said Ravà, who was later busted out by 600 government troops in a firefight.

Ravà and I stayed in touch after that first meeting. Thinking there might be a book in his family's extraordinary desert story, I wanted to see northern Chad for myself. Security advice kept changing. Ravà kept providing reassurance: "They have never had a tourist kidnapped in Chad," he said, "except me, and I'm not a tourist." Then he told me about a deal he'd struck with Ben Simpson, one of the most pioneering pilots in Africa. Tropic Air Kenya, whose helicopter division Simpson set up, operates heli safaris in remote places all over the continent.

With Ravà's ground knowledge of Chad and help from Abakar Rozi Teguil of the National Tourist Ofce (ONPTA), the logistics and permissions were now in place for a rare desert encounter. On 10 January, I flew back to N'Djamena, hoping this would be the adventure that would take me close to those extraordinary words of freedom in one of the masterpieces of desert literature: *Wind, Sand and Stars*, written by the French aviator Antoine de Saint-Exupéry who flew mail routes across the Sahara between the wars. Saint-Exupéry talks about the dangers of a thirsty imagination. "I know it's a mirage," he writes. "But suppose I feel like plunging into a mirage? Suppose I want to feel hope?" In a plane crash, his fellow survivor discovers a single orange amid the wreckage. "I lie on my back and suck the fruit, counting the shooting stars," said Saint-Exupéry. "For a moment, my happiness is infinite." I found it easy to fall for such heroic optimism.

We met on the tarmac of N'Djamena airport, Tropic Air Kenya's blue Airbus H125 packed for its month-long desert sojourn. Simpson had just come in from Kenya. A second helicopter would join us in the desert, for one of the larger client safaris that would follow (a group of eight friends), for enhanced security (so the pilots could help each other out if the circumstances required) and for wildlife conservation work, which makes up between five and ten per cent of Tropic's pan-African business every year. While in Chad, Ravà had arranged for Tropic to help with animal GPS collaring for the Sahara Conservation Fund, and some work with African Parks – two international NGOs working with the Chadian government to secure Ennedi's long-term protection.

We took to the air, Ravà and Simpson seated upfront. As we banked away from N'Djamena, a parched, endless plain of dust opened up in front. Beneath us were circles from abandoned homesteads imprinted on the earth. When we stopped to refuel in Abéché, the local security official was so glad to see a visitor he gave me a guided tour using the airport's bus. He drove me out past the windsock – the only bolt of colour for miles around – to the plane wreckage sitting to the side of the runway.

If this was getting weird, it was also only the beginning. Back in the air, Ravà told me about a time when much of Chad was under a vast inland body of water – the so-called "Caspian of the Sahara". In its more recent history, some 10,000 years ago, it was green, running with elephants, antelopes and giraffes. In Ennedi, he said, there had been enough grass to keep cattle, the evidence inscribed as petroglyphs on sandstone overhangs. Ravà talked about his personal count of rock-art sites in Ennedi (220, and rising), and how the massif had been continuously occupied by humankind since Neolithic times. These days, Ennedi is still an Eden in the middle of the Sahara. The surviving "rivers", as well as wadis, which collect seasonal rainwater, make it one of the few patches of true desert where life can exist.

It wasn't long after this conversation that the sand began to show a blush of sage green. We skimmed past natural pyramids of rock, each weathered outcrop poking out of the sea of sand, when up ahead a vast ridge appeared, the spurs reaching out like the fanned teeth of a bulldozer. As we rose higher, I could see the baked plateau stretching out into the endless horizon. We banked left, and the landscape gave way to tall, phallic pillars, to bulb-shaped protuberances. We banked right, and it changed to 1,000 narrow spires. We flew low along riverbeds, turning in pirouettes around lonely columns backlit by the slow-sinking sun.

The euphoria was almost overwhelming as we arrived in what felt like the navel of another universe: a sheltered circle of honeyed sandstone cliffs at the centre of which stood a crescent of elegant white tents, and a single, open-sided mess tent full of rugs, leather cushions and lanterns. It was here, at a long table, that Ravà and Simpson would draw up the next day's plans with Abderaman Dellei, one of Ravà's Toubou guides: skinny as a rake, clad in a leather jacket whatever the temperature.

I loved Warda Camp – opened in 2018 and newly upgraded this year, created by SVS Tchad and perfect in its simplicity: a thick duvet, a fly swat, a soft light for reading, an iron trunk and seagrass carpet, with hot showers shielded by canvas to the rear of each room. We ate fresh salads and barbecued meats; the bread tasted of Tuscany, and the wines were good. At night, we drank mossy Scotch whiskies around a campfire of slow-burning acacia wood.

Each day brought a different expedition – flying, hiking, picnicking above a 60-m-deep ravine. We walked the length of Bachikele, one of Ennedi's most important oases, where locals gathered with herds of camels, goats and sheep. The nomads dried their clothes on the roots of *Rauvolfia caffra* trees, the water as clear as tears. Then a dramatic shift in perspective when Simpson flew us with artful precision up narrow valleys, as if he were threading a needle of rock with his nimble 2.25-tonne machine. Ravà would point his finger, we'd land and find rock art – sometimes new even to him – in the nooks and crannies. Ravà identified a rogue evergreen tree, native to the Central African Republic, rooted in an oasis. "The plants tell a long story about Saharan journeys," he said, "how places like Ennedi functioned as rare refuges between the Gulf of Guinea on the shores of West Africa and the Gulf of Sinai on the east."

When we landed at Abayke, we wandered through an ancient ironworks, the clumps of smelt lying on the sand as if the people had just got up and left. Their stoves, which could be as old as 3,500 years, were still sitting in the drifts. There are stories of a last giraffe seen here in the 1950s, an oryx in the 1980s. When Ravà showed us an image of a rhino painted some 4,000 to 5,000 years before Christ – scribed in ochre, milk and albumin, on a part of the plateau you could only reach by helicopter or a ten-day camel trek – I felt keenly aware of what was already lost. Simpson saw it diferently: "Imagine what else is out there, and how much there is still to be discovered."

He was right. There were Dorcas gazelles, olive baboons, Nubian bustards and, if my eye could have reached deep enough into the canyon, the last of the Sahara's desert crocodiles. There was life where I'd expected only dust. In a graveyard of Libyan tanks, their gun turrets sticking out of the sand like submarine periscopes from swells of sea, we found unspent ammunition – relics of the 1987 Battle of Bir Kora, when Gaddafi sent in a 1,500-strong armoured task force and T-55 tanks, only to be pushed back by the Chadian army in Toyota pickups. Among makeshift graves, including the skulls of men barely concealed by slates of rock, were footprints from an animal: tiny pricks of life that the sandstorms hadn't yet erased.

And then, the moment it all made sense: the 45-km-long Koboue Abyss. In any other country, this would have the status of a national icon. In Chad, it exists undisturbed. We hovered over the gully's neck. Beneath us, a waterfall tumbled into a pool of blue.

"The first time I saw that waterfall I cried," said Ravà. I looked at him, and wondered about the man the desert makes. In my notepad are scribbled lines from Wilfred Thesiger when he ventured to Tibesti in 1938: "In the desert I had found a freedom unattainable in civilisation; a life unhampered by possessions." When Ravà was with his kidnappers – one of whom he's still in touch with – he said he finally understood the source of Toubou strength: in their extreme isolation, they felt no fear. The desert isn't romantic, said Ravà; you survive it by being ruthlessly pragmatic, by being able to be alone.

Except there was more to it than that. When I saw the Ennedi landscape for the first time, it struck me with the force of paradise. I found it profoundly moving that its beauty could still affect a man who had been brought up under its burning sun. Chad is not for everyone: risk is a very personal thing. But as I write this in isolation in England, Chad's magnificent desert is a place to which I long to return.

Source: Sophy Roberts, 2020, *Into the Unknown*; also published as *Splendid Isolation: A Trip to Remotest Chad*; *Financial Times*, March 2020. Used under licence from *The Financial Times*. All Rights Reserved.

LONG WALK TO FREEDOM

Emily Garthwaite

For *Suitcase* magazine
September 2020

It's dawn in Akre, an ancient town hoisted against a mountainside and encircled by sun-soaked sage grasslands. I'm being ushered from the main square towards an entanglement of walkways through the bazaar, and I'm not alone. Carts loaded with apples, dates and parsley, under which dozing cats rest, are heaved into position as the first distant sounds of motorbike horns flare. Smoke flees from roadside tea shops teeming with aged men and ashtrays, while young boys hurry past me laden with stacks of freshly baked bread. Led by Laween, my Kurdish-Syrian guide, and my hungry stomach, we enter a delightfully small restaurant discreetly carved into the bazaar, fit only for ten or so visitors. Our beaming host carries a tray of piping hot sugared tea as he stumbles across a floor littered with crushed walnut shells. He is followed by a younger man who covers our table with fresh bread, wild honey, cheese and tahini as an audience of elderly moustached men look on from the narrow doorway, cigarettes lolling from their mouths. This is the start of our walking journey across the Kurdistan Region of Iraq. After all, only good can come from a large breakfast at the beginning of a day's walking.

Until recently I had never thought of myself as a walker, but rather as someone who liked to take a walk. My gentle excursions through the depths of the English countryside have mostly been in solitude, punctuated only by extended breaks and by getting agreeably lost in and among woodland and lakesides for many miles at a time. As a photojournalist, though, I have been expected to walk. Most memorably I walked the world's largest annual pilgrimage, Arbae'en, through Iraq in 2017 and 2018. It was there that I met my partner Leon McCarron, a man who has singularly made a living from simply walking – or as he puts it, "human-powered journeys". He fondly told me about the mystical northerly reaches of Iraq and his longing to walk there again with me. And so, presented with the opportunity and with Leon's encouragement, I found myself walking from west to east across the Kurdistan Region of Iraq at the end of 2019.

Today there are over 25 million Kurds across Syria, Turkey, Iran and Iraq, a fifth of whom live in Iraq. After the fall of Saddam Hussain in 2003, Kurds were granted an opportunity to establish control over their mountainous territory, which exists in the autonomous locality of Iraq. Driven by oil-fuelled optimism, they transformed the region, building shopping malls, skyscrapers, bars and even a ski resort. The youth still remain optimistic about the future their forefathers fought for now that there is relative stability and security has returned to the area. The Kurdish region has been bombed, evacuated and resurrected, a site of displacement for hundreds of years as well as a place of trauma, newly ploughed land and intangible hope. Presently the greatest threat facing the region is not conflict, as many are led to believe, but rather globalisation. More than ever, traditions and heritage are on the verge of collapse – and these are the very things that walking trails seek to protect.

Over the past two years the Abraham Path Initiative, an NGO based out of Harvard, has carved the first cross-cultural long-distance walking trail, which sweeps from the west to the east of Iraqi-Kurdistan. It believes that by building cultural capital in rural communities, the path will encourage economic development and further peacebuilding. I have also witnessed the desire to experience meaningful, authentic trips to places that few have gone before becoming an increasing trend in global tourism. The trail requires a large group of collaborators to make this possible. From drivers and translators to guides, mine advisors, guest-house owners and local restaurants, the trail offers an in-depth understanding of not only the landscape, but also its culture and history as told by locals. We follow the walkways of Neanderthals alongside shepherds in the meadow grass lowlands and along humble tributaries leading to the Great Zab River, towards the ancient Assyrian hilltop town of Amedi. We travel on foot with Yazidi pilgrims towards the mountain valley temple of Lalish, the holiest site for the Yazidi faith, and wander down roads built by Saddam Hussein. Later on as part of an assignment, I walk inch by inch with de-miners from Mines Advisory Group, which is restoring the land and saving lives in a country that has more than eight million active landmines lying ominously only inches below the soil. As a photographer one has to move slowly enough to encounter chance and to see the world fully and with clarity. This is what walking allows; the opportunity to be humbled, to better understand the world and to be questioning. It's about the spaces in-between, rather than the walk itself.

Until I met Ahmed, I'd never been taught to walk. I never knew there was more than one way to move your legs. Ahmed is part of the Peshmerga military, which literally translates to "those who face death", and lives in the most easterly snow-capped point of the Kurdistan Region of Iraq. At almost 70 years old, Ahmed walks as though carried by the wind and held by the mountains that surround us. I, on the other hand, feel as though my limbs are rooted in the soil as we climb higher. He tells me with handfuls of hopeful words and encouragement, "Swing your arms, lean, follow me! You're a proud walker, Emily. A great walker."

Ahmed's story is one of sacrifice and, I learn as I continue to walk over the following weeks, one sadly shared by all who live here. These tales lace the trails and are part of the very fabric of the land. The day after Ahmed and his wife Fatemah married, the war began. They hid in a cave only minutes from their family home for a month, which we visit during the midday heat. We only intend to stop at his house for tea, but unsurprisingly Fatemah has prepared a feast for us. Mountains of fresh salads and pomegranate molasses lie on a thick tapestry rug alongside chickpea soup, dates and hand-made bread. I turn to Ahmed and ask what it means to him to walk. "In the war, I was walking during a dictatorship and in a place of pain. Now when I walk, I walk without the pain. It's heaven. How could this not be heaven? Before, we had no right to breathe, but now we're free. Imagine, at the top of this mountain, where we're walking, was an Iraqi military base. Now you see they're free. The mountains are free, and we sacrificed our blood to be free. I sacrificed my blood. And here I am, walking again."

This isn't my only encounter with the Peshmerga. Nights later, we enter a small village suspended like a luminous jewel among the Zagros mountains. I'm led barefoot into a narrow sitting room, seemingly fumigated with men's cologne and cigarette smoke and lined with the obligatory part-peeling, part-squeaking faux-leather sofas that are found in all Kurdish households. I'd come to understand that upon entering one of these rooms, you would be expected to stay with your hosts for a minimum of two hours, consume plenty of black tea, and be routinely offered plates of fruit and cigarettes. It's a rite of passage and one I have learned to speed up over the years, usually by hurrying into the women's quarters with a camera. This evening, however, I stay seated. Lit by a single naked bulb and a large TV screen churning out dramatic Kurdish music videos, a smiling Peshmerga general looks out from his large desk. "Welcome to Kurdistan! We are so glad to see you here in this beautiful land; a land made for walking! Please, join us for dinner!" It's then I notice the bleating sheep through the window nearest to me have disappeared. Only the rope remains. Hours later, mutton is on the menu for our evening meal. The power cuts and we're lit by the orange glow of gas heaters and phone lights dancing as their owners shuffle across the floor seeking out food. We sleep in modest rooms that evening, as we do most nights, and I think deeply about how impactful simply walking is, both for myself and for those living along the trail.

It's not just the military who encourage walking, but the youth too. Every weekend thousands of young Kurds take to the hillsides for hiking trips. Arez, a mechanic during the week and mountaineer at the weekend, is one such individual. "The outdoors plays a huge role in surviving tough situations. I lost a lot of dreams when I left Baghdad, as well as friends and family. I was working at least two jobs from the age of sixteen and studying all the while. I had to survive to handle these situations. I think the outdoors was the escape – the mountains gave me purpose. It's like a free therapist. When I'm at the top of a mountain, I think about nothing. I feel reborn and prepared for life." I personally came to Kurdistan bruised from years of working in the field. In many ways, I sought safety in a land that has been bruised and beaten too. I found an affinity with its walkways and mountainsides. The landscape and people healed me and restored my faith in humanity. More simply, I realised that a lot of good can be done by a walk, a large breakfast and the company of kind strangers. As a photojournalist, I often find myself in strange and seemingly disconnected scenarios around the globe, but each is connected by walking and the people I meet along the way. How very familiar it is to embed myself within a family, to experience a temporary inclusion, a home, a site of love, and then to disappear.

For the first time, in Kurdistan I felt compelled to stay – and so at the end of 2019 I moved to the city of Erbil in the heart of Iraqi Kurdistan. Still, it is my job to be a familiar stranger, to suck out people's poison and meet their inner child, peering from behind their ribcage in all its imperfect perfection. I am both a keeper of secrets and a teller of stories, who, for now at least, can be found hiking in the Kurdish countryside at weekends.

At this time of immense uncertainty and new global order, one can only hope that old barriers and misconceptions break down and that we open the way for new forms of travel. It is time for other regions and countries to take their rightful place as desirable destinations. We must move beyond closed borders and narrow minds to a more accepting global society. Sometimes it takes a monumental crisis to see what we value, want and need – but perhaps the answer lies right beneath our feet.

AUTHOR BIOGRAPHIES

Leon McCarron

Leon McCarron's words come from slow, immersive journeys. He has travelled over 30,000 miles on foot and by bike and boat, and tells stories big and small through the voices of those on the ground. He has presented two films for the BBC and is a Fellow of the Royal Geographical Society. His journalism has appeared in *National Geographic*, *Smithsonian* magazine, *New Scientist* and *Noema*. His third book, *Wounded Tigris: A River Journey through the Cradle of Civilisation* will be published in late 2022. Leon lives in Erbil in the Kurdistan region of Iraq. leonmccarron.com

Oliver Smith

Oliver Smith is a London-based travel writer, working regularly for *The Times*, *The Financial Times* and *Outside* magazine among others. He has won numerous awards including AITO Travel Writer of the Year, Consumer Travel Writer of the Year at the Travel Media Awards and Gold at the Lowell Thomas Awards from the Society of American Travel Writers.

Solange Hando

Solange Hando has contributed articles to over 100 titles, from travel and lifestyle magazines to newspapers and in-flights. Whether it's local culture, soft adventure – trekking, safaris, inland waterways – city breaks, mountains and beaches, wildlife or natural wonders, ideas keep bouncing wherever she goes, be it the South of France or the

Himalayas. Add *Bhutan Pocket Guide* (Berlitz/Insight), *Journeys of a Lifetime* (National Geographic), *Be a Travel Writer* (John Hunt), public speaking and workshops, and this is just a glimpse of her amazing life. travelwriters.co.uk/personal-pages/solange-hando/

Ash Bhardwaj

Ash Bhardwaj has built a career by challenging the conventions of travel journalism. His work focuses on the interplay of travel, current affairs, identity, privilege, race, historical narrative and the environment. He has written for all the UK's leading travel magazines and newspapers, and writes a monthly column – Lost & Found – for *The Telegraph*. He regularly reports for BBC Radio Four and the World Service, co-hosts The First Mile travel podcast, and is a visiting lecturer in Journalism at City, University of London. ashbhardwaj.com, @ashbhardwaj

Charlie Walker

Charlie Walker is a British explorer and writer specialising in long-distance, human-powered expeditions visiting remote peoples. He has travelled over 50,000 miles by bicycle, foot, horse, ski, kayak and dugout canoe. He is a Fellow of the Royal Geographical Society and a three-time recipient of the Transglobe Expedition Trust's "Mad but Marvellous" award. His work has featured in a range of publications including *The Sunday Times, The Telegraph, The Sun, Wanderlust, Geographical* and *Sidetracked* magazine, as well as BBC Radio 4 and the World Service. He has written two books about his experiences. cwexplore.com, @cwexplore

Jack Palfrey

A former Digital Editor at Lonely Planet, Jack is a Cardiff-based freelance journalist focusing on producing entertaining and enlightening – typically environmentally-tinged – travel stories for publications including *BBC Travel* and *National Geographic Traveller*. Away from work he's a sucker for a good adventure, a good ale and good alliteration (and also Indian food but that sort of ruins the wordplay). jackpalfreyfreelance.com

William Gray

Zoologist, writer and photographer, Will has 30 years' experience writing for newspapers, magazines and conservation organisations. His writing career began when he was 23, following the publication of *Coral Reefs & Islands: The Natural History of a Threatened Paradise*. More recent titles have included *Family Wildlife Adventures*, *Wildlife Travel* and *Travel with Kids*. He has won over 20 awards for journalism, including AITO Travel Writer of the Year and BGTW Travel Photographer of the Year. His photography is represented by AWL Images and he runs photography workshops in the UK. Will's passion for wild places has taken him from Svalbard to the Serengeti, Madagascar to the Galapagos Islands. william-gray.co.uk, @willgrayphotography

Tim Hannigan

Tim Hannigan is an author and academic from the far west of Cornwall. He began his travel writing career as a journalist based in Indonesia, and he has worked on guidebooks covering destinations across Southeast Asia for Insight, DK Eyewitness and Tuttle. He has also written several narrative history books, including *Murder in the Hindu Kush* and *A Brief History of Indonesia*.

His most recent book, *The Travel Writing Tribe*, explores the debates around contemporary travel literature through encounters with some of its best-known practitioners. He is currently working on a new book about Cornwall, due for publication in 2023. timhannigan.com, @Tim_Hannigan

Lizzie Pook

Lizzie Pook is an award-winning freelance journalist and author, covering wildlife and adventure travel for publications including *Condé Nast Traveller*, *Rough Guides*, *Lonely Planet*, *Evening Standard*, *The Telegraph* and *The Times*. Her assignments have taken her to some of the most remote parts of the world, from the uninhabited east coast of Greenland in search of narwhals and polar bears, to the haunting mountains of the Trans-Himalayas to track endangered and elusive snow leopards. Her first novel *Moonlight and the Pearler's Daughter* was published by Pan Macmillan in March 2022. She lives in London.

Adrian Phillips

Adrian Phillips runs Bradt Travel Guides – the world's largest independent guidebook publisher – as well as writing and broadcasting for outlets including the BBC, ITV, Sky, *The Telegraph*, *The Times* and *National Geographic Traveller*. He covers everything from city breaks to excursions into the rainforest, and spends much of his time lost and uncomfortable. Awards for his work include Travel Writer of the Year (BGTW Awards, AITO Awards), Consumer Writer of the Year (Travel Media Awards), Magazine Writer of the Year (LATA Awards) and Broadcaster of the Year (BGTW Awards). adrianjphillips.com, @adrianphillips1

Antonia Quirke

Antonia Quirke is a British film critic, interviewer, and travel writer. She presents programmes about film on BBC TV and radio 4, and is a familiar voice on the World Service with her travel reports for From Our Own Correspondent. Contributing editor to *Condé Nast Traveller*, her books include the Modern Classic on the movie *JAWS*, and the memoir *Madame Depardieu and the Beautiful Strangers*, which was described by Clive James as "a comic success on a dizzy level".

Stephanie Cavagnaro

Stephanie Cavagnaro is a freelance travel journalist and editor. She is the former Deputy Editor of *National Geographic Traveller* (UK), where she worked for eight years. In addition to being a frequent *National Geographic Traveller* (UK) contributor, Stephanie has also written for titles including *Travel + Leisure*, *The Telegraph*, *The Independent* and *ABTA Magazine*. In 2017, Stephanie was shortlisted for the AITO Young Travel Writer of the Year award. She grew up in New York and has recently moved with her husband and two small children from London to Somerset, where she is writing her first novel. @stacava

Nick Hunt

Nick Hunt has walked and written across much of Europe. He is the author of three travel books – *Outlandish: Walking Europe's Unlikely Landscapes*, *Where the Wild Winds Are* and *Walking the Woods and the Water* – as well as a work of "gonzo ornithology", *The Parakeeting of London*. His articles and features have been published in *The Guardian Travel, Emergence, The Economist, New Internationalist* and other publications. He is an editor and co-director at the Dark

Mountain Project, and also works as an editorial consultant for the John Murray Journeys series. nickhuntscrutiny.com

Jessica J. Lee

Jessica J. Lee is an author, environmental historian, and winner of the Hilary Weston Writers' Trust Prize for Nonfiction, the Boardman Tasker Award for Mountain Literature, the Banff Mountain Book Award, and the RBC Taylor Prize Emerging Writer Award. She is the author of two books of nature writing: *Turning* (2017) and *Two Trees Make a Forest* (2019), which was shortlisted for Canada Reads 2021. She has a PhD in Environmental History and Aesthetics and is the founding editor of The Willowherb Review. She is a researcher at the University of Cambridge.

Emma Thomson

Emma has been hooked on all things travel since the age of 14, when she would sneakily rip pages out of ageing copies of *National Geographic* in the school library to add to her travel scrapbook. Happily, life came full circle when she was invited to speak at Nat Geo headquarters in Washington DC in 2017. Prior to this, she spent six years as Commissioning Editor at Bradt Travel Guides, before leaving to join a world-first expedition crossing Namibia's Skeleton Coast unsupported. Since then Emma has specialised in covering countries recovering from natural disaster or political upheaval to help travellers regain trust in these places. An experienced speaker and regular travel-writing panellist, she has featured on BBC Radio 4's *From Our Own Correspondent* and presented for TV. ethomson. co.uk, @emmathomsontravels

Lilly Ryzebol and Andrew Ryzebol

Andrew Ryzebol began freediving on the Great Lakes and was certified in the cold Canadian waters. Over the years, he has developed expertise on local Ontario dive sites with some of the harshest conditions. Andrew freedives year-round in Canada, which provides unique experiences and challenges with each season. Lilly Ryzebol is a competitive freediver with one Canadian National Record. Lilly fell in love with the water after losing her mother to cancer and freediving helped her overcome her fear of the water from a drowning incident as a child. Her passion for travel has opened many opportunities to dive shipwrecks, caves and underwater mazes and to try ice diving with her husband Andrew, all with just one breath.

Karen Edwards

Karen Edwards is an editor and writer from London who specializes in responsible tourism, sustainable living and emotional well-being. She writes for a variety of national and international titles, including *High Life* by British Airways, *Balance*, *Breathe*, *Grazia*, *Metro*, *The Independent* and *Time Out*. Karen inherited her love for the planet at a young age while travelling with her parents. Since then, she's been fortunate to explore many regions, from Antarctica and the Russian Arctic to Indonesia and the Pacific Islands. She lives between London and South Australia with her marine biologist fiancé. karenedwards.co.uk, @KarenNEdwards_writer.

Douglas Rogers

Zimbabwe-born Douglas Rogers is an award-winning author, journalist and travel writer. He has reported from more than 50 countries and his work has appeared in *The Telegraph, The Guardian, New York Times, Wall Street Journal, Travel + Leisure, Condé Nast Traveller* and elsewhere. He is the author of the acclaimed *The Last Resort: A Memoir of Mischief* and *Mayhem on a Family Farm in Africa* (2010) and the non-fiction political thriller *Two Weeks in November: The Astonishing Untold Story of the Operation that Toppled Mugabe* (2019). He lives in Virginia with his wife and two children. douglasrogers.org

Amelia Duggan

With journalism awards including Specialist Travel Writer of the Year and Young Travel Writer of the Year to her name, Amelia's adventures have taken her to the four corners of the earth, from visiting Maya temples in Mexico and living root bridges in Meghalaya to the nightclubs of Miami and the shores of Lake Malawi. Her work has appeared in publications including *The Times, The Telegraph* and *Evening Standard*. Following a formative stint as a reporter in Santiago, Chile in her early twenties, Amelia returned to her hometown of London where she is now deputy editor of the award-winning *National Geographic Traveller* (UK) magazine. ameliaduggan.com

Tharik Hussain

Tharik Hussain is an author, travel writer and journalist specialising in Muslim heritage and culture. His debut book, *Minarets in the Mountains; A Journey into Muslim Europe,* was nominated for the 2021 Baillie Gifford Prize for Nonfiction. Tharik is also the co-author of several Lonely Planet guidebooks, including *Oman, UAE and the Arabian Peninsula, Best of Thailand* and *Thailand*. He is the creator of Britain's first Muslim heritage trails and award-winning radio for the

BBC World Service on America's earliest mosques. Tharik is also a Fellow at the Centre of Religion and Heritage at the University of Groningen. tharikhussain.co.uk, @_tharikhussain

James Draven

James Draven is a multi-award-winning travel journalist whose words and photographs appear in *National Geographic Traveller, The Times, The Guardian, The Independent, The Telegraph, CNN, Travel + Leisure*, and many more publications. Raised on a Kent council estate, James is an unlikely travel writer: he didn't leave the country until he was aged 20, and his GCSE English teacher considered him a lost cause. Today, James has travelled the globe from Antarctica to Zürich, and his stories have been published in English textbooks alongside works by Charles Dickens, Sir John Betjeman, Dame Agatha Christie, and Sir Arthur Conan Doyle. His school has since been bulldozed. @JamesDraven

J. R. Patterson

J. R. Patterson was born in Manitoba, Canada, in 1989, and raised on a beef and grain farm outside of Gladstone. His experiences as a farm labourer, factory worker, and musician inform much of his writing, which appears regularly in a variety of international publications. He divides his time between Canada and Portugal. jrpatterson.ca.

Noo Saro-Wiwa

Noo Saro-Wiwa is a British-Nigerian author and freelance journalist. Her first book, *Looking for Transwonderland: Travels in Nigeria* (Granta, 2012), was selected as BBC Radio 4's Book of the Week, and named a Sunday Times Travel Book of the Year in 2012. *National Geographic* and *Oprah* magazine have also listed it among their top travel books.

Her next book, *Black Ghost*, will be published by Canongate in 2023. Noo writes book reviews, travel and opinion articles for various publications, including *Condé Nast Traveller*, *The Guardian*, *The Times Literary Supplement*, *Prospect* magazine and *City AM*. @noosarowiwa (Twitter), @noo.saro.wiwa (Instagram)

Joey Tyson

Joey Tyson is a travel writer and journalist from West Yorkshire. Currently based in Milan, Italy, he writes about the environment, big walks, obscure adventures, and unusual people. His work has appeared in *The Independent, BBC Travel, Suitcase* magazine, and *The Guardian*, among others. @joeytyson27

Lola Akinmade Åkerström

Lola Akinmade Åkerström is an award-winning visual storyteller, international bestselling author, and travel entrepreneur. She has dispatched from 70+ countries and her work has been featured in *National Geographic, New York Times, The Guardian, BBC, CNN, Travel Channel, Travel + Leisure, Lonely Planet, Forbes*, and more. She has collaborated with brands such as Dove, Mercedes Benz, Intrepid Travel, Electrolux, and National Geographic Channel, to name a few. She runs Geotraveler Media Academy, dedicated to visual storytelling and helping the next generation of travel storytellers put the heart back into the craft. akinmade.com, @LolaAkinmade

Stanley Stewart

Stanley Stewart is the author of three highly acclaimed travel books and several hundred articles based on journeys across five continents. His latest book, *In the Empire of Genghis Khan*, about a thousand-mile horse ride across Mongolia, has been translated into ten languages, and was the BBC Book of the Week. He has been named Travel Writer of the Year six times and was awarded the Magazine Writer of the Year in 2008. He is a contributing editor of *Condé Nast Traveller*, and in the UK his work appears regularly in *The Sunday Times*, among others. *The Times Literary Supplement* has described him as "among the very first rank of contemporary travel writers." In 2002, he was elected a Fellow of the Royal Society of Literature.

Michelle Jana Chan

Michelle Jana Chan has spent the last 25 years writing and editing for *Vanity Fair*, *The Financial Times*, *Newsweek* and *The Telegraph*, and broadcasting for the BBC, Deutsche Welle and CNN. Her TEDx talk is "Hitchhiking, galaxies, and why travel is not bad for the planet". Her novel *Song (Unbound)* was described by Bernardine Evaristo as "a wonderfully lush and atmospheric odyssey of survival against all odds"; Elif Shafak called it "Precise, heartfelt, breathtaking". Michelle hosts The Wandering Book Collector podcast and her next book *Two Friends (And Other Stories)* will be published in 2022. linktr.ee/michellejanachan

Rae Boocock

Rae is a writer, editor and grammar nerd who grew up near Blackpool, dabbled in London and washed down the coast to Brighton, where she lives with her three cats. Her words have appeared everywhere from local newspapers to *Livingetc* and ads on the underground. After years crafting and subbing copy for *Suitcase* magazine and creative studio, she joined the team at words-first agency Sonder & Tell. When she's not getting lost in a library book, she's getting lost on the South Downs, by the sea or crocheting with a cuppa. @raeishungry

Sophy Roberts

Sophy Roberts is based in West Dorset. She is a regular contributor on travel to *The Financial Times*, among other titles. Sophy's writing focuses on remote places, often overlooked in the news – the Democratic Republic of Congo, Chad, Tajikistan. Her first book, *The Lost Pianos of Siberia*, was a *Sunday Times* Book of the Year (2020) and is published in 13 languages worldwide. lostpianosofsiberia.com

Emily Garthwaite

Emily Garthwaite is an award-winning photojournalist, Forbes 30 Under 30, Leica Ambassador and storyteller. She has walked over 1,000 km through Iraq and Iran in order to document environmental and humanitarian stories focusing on transhumance, climate change, and our coexistence with the natural world. She has exhibited her work internationally, including at the World Economic Forum, EXPO 2020 in UAE and in the UK, at Leica Mayfair Gallery, South Bank Centre, Somerset House and The Natural History Museum. Her work has been published in *Smithsonian, Sunday Times Magazine, NPR, The Guardian* and *Vanity Fair*. emilygarthwaite.com, @emilygarthwaite

THE LONGLIST

In early 2021, we asked travel writers around the world to submit their best work published in UK magazines, newspapers and online publications between the years 2000 and 2021 for a chance to be included in *The Best British Travel Writing of the 21st Century*. The response was incredible – we received hundreds of submissions from some of the most talented writers in the business. Unfortunately we could only choose 30 stories, but we'd like to extend our congratulations to the following writers who made the longlist:

Why Armenians Love Strangers by Ben Lerwill (*BBC Travel*)

An Exhilarating Train Journey Across the Sahara by Alastair Gill (*BBC Travel*)

Home is Where the Pasture Is by Kate Eshelby (*The Independent*)

Life with the Ice Men by Sara Evans (*Sunday Telegraph*)

Happy to Be Sad by Max Wooldridge (*The Observer*)

In the Land of the Lone Ranger by Aaron Millar (*The Times*)

Game Face by Kate Eshelby (*Condé Nast Traveller*)

The Land that Time Forgot: Hiking the Bale Mountains, Ethiopia by Lizzie Pook (*Suitcase* magazine)

The Enema Within by Ian Belcher (*The Guardian*)

Paradise Unplugged by Sophy Roberts (*Financial Times*)

Riders on the Storm by Mark Stratton (*The Telegraph*)

Heartbeats by Markus Torgeby (*Sidetracked* magazine)

The Last Overland: Retracing an Epic 1955 Road Trip from London to Singapore by Alex Bescoby (*The Telegraph*)

Dawn Chorus by John Malathronas (*The Sunday Times*)

Pork, Lemongrass – and the Laos Factor by Claire Boobbyer (*Sunday Telegraph*)

The Wheels Deal by Mike Unwin (*Travel Africa* magazine)

Lemur the Merrier by Meera Dattani (*Evening Standard*)

THANK YOU

This book would not have been possible without the immense talent and support of everyone involved. In particular, I'd like to extend my deepest thanks to the incredible writers and photographers included in this anthology. Thank you for showing us the world through your eyes, and for allowing us to republish your work. Believe me when I say that it's a huge privilege to share and celebrate your passion for storytelling with the readers of this book.

I'd also like to thank my wonderful co-editors, Levison Wood, Monisha Rajesh and Simon Willmore. Without them, choosing just thirty stories out of the hundreds of submissions we received would have felt like an impossible task. To this day, they continue to generously support the book with live Instagram broadcasts, speaking events and countless retweets. I can only hope you've enjoyed being part of this as much as I have.

To the hundreds of writers who submitted their work, thank you. We couldn't include everyone, but please know that your stories made us fall in love with travel writing, and the world, all over again. Thank you also to the amazing publications that originally published the stories that feature in this anthology, and who continue to champion brilliant travel storytelling from around the world. Without you, this book, and travel writing as we know it, would not exist.

A huge thank you to our generous sponsors, battleface and the British Guild of Travel Writers, for their enthusiasm and support of British travel writing. This book would not have been possible without your backing.

I'd also like to extend a big thank you to the Summersdale team and my editor, Debbie Chapman, for their hard work over the past year. Debbie, thank you for believing in this book from the very beginning. Your patience, diligence and infectious positivity have been instrumental in getting *The Best British Travel Writing of the 21st Century* over the finish line. A special thank you also to Summersdale's wonderful marketing and publicity executive, Jasmin Burkitt, who has worked tirelessly to make sure this anthology reaches as many readers as possible.

Finally, I'd like to thank you – the reader – for choosing to read this book. Your support of the travel writing genre means the world, and I can only hope that these pages inspire you to dream bigger and adventure deeper for years to come.

Jessica Vincent

A WORD FROM OUR SPONSORS

battleface®

We believe that travel has a positive impact on people's lives. Travel helps people better understand other cultures, come together, and embrace diversity.

Whether visiting friends and family, experiencing new places and cultures, or simply sipping from coconuts at the beach, people moving from place to place are likely to face obstacles.

Situations can change quickly. That's why battleface's insurance plans continue working, even in destinations under government travel advisories.

With battleface to back them up, travellers can face challenges with confidence. For people headed around the corner or around the world, battleface helps explorers keep their eyes on the road.

Just as the world belongs to everyone on it, so does the information about it. That's why we've created resources, from podcast interviews to safety-tip blog posts, for curious travellers with a variety of needs and interests:

- Watch *When it Hits the Fan* for podcasts about how adventurers got in and out of travel trouble, including an interview with *The Best British Travel Writing of the 21st Century* author, Leon McCarron.

- Research or plan a trip based on the latest health and safety information on the battleface Travel Hub page.
- Read the battleface blog for articles about safety tips, top destinations, interviews, photo essays and more.

You can also use battleface to invest in your next destination. battleface contributes to projects that enrich communities all over the world, including Kiva, an international non-profit that facilitates crowdfunded loans for people underserved by financial institutions.

For daily updates, tips, and inspiration, follow @battlefacePlan on social media or check out our website battleface.com.

The British Guild of Travel Writers (BGTW) is a community of almost 300 accredited writers, photographers, bloggers and broadcasters based all over the world. It is the trusted body for independent comment and expert content on British, Irish and global travel. Founded in 1960, the BGTW turned 60 years old in 2020 – that's six decades at the forefront of the travel media industry. All applicants are screened and interviewed, and all members abide by a strict code of conduct to ensure they report on matters fairly, accurately and sustainably.

BGTW members receive numerous benefits such as access to professional development webinars and meetings, networking and social events, an international press card, exclusive discounts and press trip invitations, and the chance to enter awards schemes.

If you are British or Irish, live in the British Isles or produce travel content for British publications, the BGTW Board would love to hear from you! Go to bgtw.org for more information and please follow the BGTW on social media: Twitter.com/TravWriters, Facebook.com/TravWriters and Instagram.com/TravWriters.

COPYRIGHT
ACKNOWLEDGEMENTS

pp.250–255 Emily Garthwaite has asserted her right to be identified as a Contributor to the Work in accordance with sections 77 and 78 of the Copyright, Designs and Patents Act 1988. Story first published in *Suitcase* magazine, Volume 31: Freedom, reproduced with kind permission of *Suitcase* magazine.

PHOTOGRAPHY ACKNOWLEDGEMENTS

pp.274–277 © Joe Howard. Originally published alongside *Current Affairs* by Rae Boocock in *Suitcase* magazine

Page numbers below refer to the plates section

p.1 © Kevin Faingnaert. Originally published alongside *The Old Country* by Karen Edwards in *High Life* magazine

pp.2–3 © Emily Garthwaite. Originally published alongside *The Night Train* by Leon McCarron in *Suitcase* magazine

pp.4–5 © Geoff Coombs. Originally published alongside *Change in a Single Breath* by Lilly Ryzebol with Andrew Ryzebol in *Sidetracked* magazine

pp.6–7 © Emily Garthwaite. Originally published alongside *Long Walk to Freedom* by Emily Garthwaite in *Suitcase* magazine

p.8 © Archie Leeming. Originally published alongside *Pirogue: Descent of the River Lulua, DRC* by Charlie Walker in *Sidetracked* magazine